Keto Instant Pot Cookbook

Keto Instant Pot Cookbook

Delicious, Quick & Easy Keto Instant Pot Recipes to Lose Weight and Live a Healthy Life!(Instant Pot Keto Recipes To Help You Save Time & Money)

Elena Jennifer

TABLE OF CONTENTS

Introduction:

Most of us think that cooking can be fast or gourmet, and there is no third possibility. On the other hand, the majority of people think that food cannot be healthy and delicious all at the same time. Yes, we are right; there are recipes that require hours of preparation. If you don't have extra time on your hands and you are feeling a little overwhelmed, it can be daunting for you. This is the reason why we rather opt for a portion of take-out food. If we have to follow a specific diet, it makes things even more difficult!

Notwithstanding this truth, there is a practical solution out there. It's time for a paradigm shift that will make a change in your life! An Instant Pot offers delicious, healthy, gourmet and quick meals at one time. Furthermore, if you follow a Ketogenic diet, you can cook your favorite food in the Instant Pot easily and effortlessly. You can get benefits of the Ketogenic diet and pressure cooking plus the extra time for your loved ones. It is a win-win situation!

What is the Keto Diet?

"A Ketogenic diet may be a diet that derives most of its calories from fat and solely a tiny low variety of calories from carbohydrates. The diet forces the body to burn fats instead of carbohydrates for energy. Normally, the carbohydrates you eat are becoming aldohexose within the body, which is used for energy around the body and in the brain. The liver will use hold on fat and also the fat you eat for energy. Stored fat is broken into 2 elements, fatty acids, and ketone bodies. Ketone bodies power the brain instead of glucose. This state of getting loads of organic compound bodies in your blood is termed symptom."

When I discovered a keto lifestyle, something about it really inspired me to do detailed research. I need a lot of articles and studies, seeing real people getting real and great results; then, I put theory into practice and Voila! I did it! And I did it well! A month after starting this amazing lifestyle, my life completely changed.

I started following a Ketogenic diet with a daily calorie breakdown of 5% carbs, 20% protein, and 75% fats. I also tried to stay within my calorie needs. It is not difficult since a common symptom of this diet is the feeling of fullness. Appetite suppression may be linked to a higher intake of fat and protein. My ultimate goal was to boost the body's metabolism to speed up my weight loss.

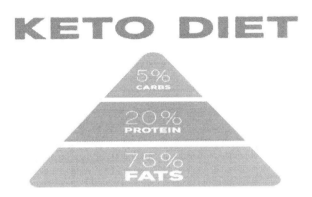

Besides being in ketosis, I tried to make some changes to help rev up my metabolism. Some of these changes include eating a good breakfast, doing simple exercises to build muscles, eating protein with every meal, drinking green tea, and adding hot peppers to my meals.

Once I reached my ideal weight, I tried to rotate very low carbohydrate days with higher carbohydrate days so I can say that simple plan works for me. Alternatively, you can keep on with your keto lifestyle, but you can eat a little more food for weight maintenance. You can add a little more protein but keep carbs low. You can add more carbs only before and after workouts. It is advisable to go slowly, and raise your daily carb limit by 10 to 10 grams for a week or two, and stick with Paleo foods. In this phase, you can eat carbs that are nutrient-dense and fiber-rich such as carrots, peppers, potatoes, turnips, pears, bananas, oranges, and strawberries. Another great way to maintain your goal weight is to combine intermittent fasting with muscle-gaining keto. The key is just to find that perfect amount of food for the body, age, and activity level. Most people, including me, do not have to be in ketosis to stay at a healthy weight, as long as they stick with a low-carb diet such as Paleo, LCHF or low-carb Mediterranean diet. Almost four years into keto, I am maintaining my ideal weight, feeling freedom from food like the one I have never had before. Pro Tip: Choose nutrient-packed foods that can satiate you easier, and automatically, you will eat less.

Benefits of the Keto Diet:

1. When you cut carbohydrates; you are going to be losing weight. There are some studies that have shown that people who are on diets, where there are less carbs being eaten, lose weight faster. A reason for this is because a low carb diet tends to get rid of the extra water that is in your body.

Since the insulin levels are lowered; your kidneys will be shredding the excess sodium leading to rapid weight loss in the first few weeks of the diet.

2. Lowering how often you eat protein will make it to where you can take in the proper qualities of diet, instead of overdoing it or under doing it like many people tend to do. At some point in time, you will place your body in ketosis and you will want less food which is going to lower the glucose in your system.

3. The fat that is in your body will be used to fuel it so you can make it through the day. This is not going to happen if you are eating a lot of carbohydrates or if you are on a high carbohydrate diet.
The more carbs that you put into your body; the more energy you will feel, but when your body reaches ketosis, then you have to force your body to become efficient by fueling itself to use the fat as energy.

4. Since your body is not going to have all of the insulin in it, you will allow your hormones to stabilize as they are released in your body. There are some hormones that are going to be affected such as the growth hormones.
5. Not all body fat is going to be the same; and with a low carbohydrate intake you are going to realize that most of your fat is going to come from your abdominal cavity. The fact that you are going to lose more of is going to be the visceral fat that will hang out around your organs, and with a lot of fat there it is going to drive inflammation up. This is one of the biggest drivers for the metabolic dysfunctions that we see today.
But a low-fat diet is going to get rid of a lot of the harmful fat that we put into our body. Not only that but it can help with other health issues that you may be experiencing.

6. Ketones that enter your body during ketosis will make it to where you are not hungry as often. This means you eat less.

7. Since low carbohydrate diets are high in fat; that is going to increase your HDL level, otherwise known as good cholesterol.

8. There have been studies that show that when you reduce your carbs you will also be lowering your blood pressure which is one of the biggest risk factors for a lot of diseases that you see now a day.

9. The lower your triglyceride levels are; the lower your risk for heart disease will be.

10. To lower blood sugar and insulin, you will reduce your carbohydrate consumption which may even be able to reverse type II diabetes.

Instant Pot Structure:

Traditional pressure cookers were made for stovetops while electric pressure cookers, like the Instant Pot, run on electricity. An Instant Pot has a pressure cooking container (inner pot), an electric heating element (base), and temperature or pressure sensors. These parts allow you to throw in the ingredients, set the type of food you are cooking and the cooking duration, and them leave it to let the Instant Pot do the rest.

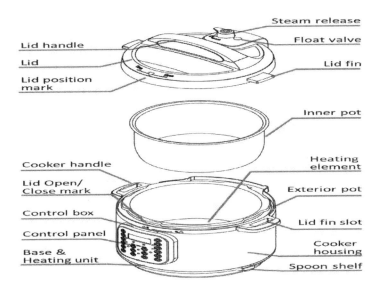

Over time, electric pressure cookers have been developed to do a wide range of functions including braising, sautéing, simmering, slow cooking, steaming, stewing, rice cooking, warming, and many others by simply using a variety of temperature, pressure and duration combinations.

How to Use an Instant Pot:

There are many pre-programmed buttons on the Instant Pot. Here are some of the programs which yours may have.

1. **Pressure Cook/Manual-** for regular pressure cooking; you can control the temperature, pressure levels, and cook times.
2. **Soup/Broth-** for slow simmering soups.
3. **Meat/Stew-**for cooking large chunks of meat at high pressure.
4. **Bean/Chill-**for cooking beans.
5. **Cake-** for cooking very moist and dense cakes.
6. **Egg-** for cooking extra-large eggs.
7. **Sauté-** for sautéing.
8. **Slow Cook-** for replacing your slow cooker.

9. **Rice-** for cooking white rice on low pressure.
10. **Multigrain-** for cooking brown rice, wild rice, other tough whole grains.
11. **Porridge-** for making oatmeal, rice porridge (congee); or rice porridge (congee) with beans.
12. **Steam-** for steaming vegetables, seafood, and fish.
13. **Sterilize-** for sterilizing jars, baby bottles, and other utensils, pasteurizing dairy products, etc.
14. **Yogurt-** for fermenting or pasteurizing milk.
15. **Keep Warm-** for maintaining food at serving temperatures.

Benefits of an Instant Pot:

Instant Potting has many, many advantages, as cooks all over the world can attest. Check the other benefits that come with using your Instant Pot.

- Foods are cooked up to 70% faster and, since an Instant Pot uses less water, you can also save up to 70% of energy compared to traditional cooking methods.
- Pressure cooking keeps vitamins, minerals, and flavor in your food because an Instant Pot has a fully sealed cooking mechanism.
- Food is cooked above water's boiling point, killing most harmful bacteria and viruses; making Instant pots effective sterilizers.
- The Instant Pot is a device that can do many common cooking tasks. No cooking experience or skills required.
- Prep, cooking, or clean-up is a breeze. It's a multi-cooker so you only need to prepare and clean-up one cooking appliance. Cooking with Instant Pot is quick, easy, quiet, smell, steam, and heat-free.

Dos and Don'ts of the Ketogenic Diet

If you are not familiar with the keto, mistakes can be made to keep you from having good health and reaping the benefits of this diet. To enhance your success with the Ketogenic diet, here are some dos and don'ts.

1. Don'ts increase your carb intake:

The Ketogenic diet is a low-carb diet, which means you should lower your carb intake. A specific number of carbs you should have in a diet is not there. Many people follow a diet where they consume 100 to 150 grams of carbs a day. To achieve ketosis, be sure that your carbohydrate intake is low.
Most keto dieters manage the state of ketosis by consuming between 20 to 100 grams of carbs a day.

2. Don't fear fat:

If you are on a Ketogenic diet, don't be scared of fat, especially if you consume healthy fats like OOmega-3s, monounsaturated fats, and saturated fats. Fats are encouraged in the Ketogenic diet plan; a limit of 60 to 70% fat intake is best. To achieve these levels of fat, you must consume meat and healthy fats, such as olive oil, lard, butter, coconut, or alternatives on a daily basis.

3. Avoid fast food:

Not having time to cook may make you turn of fast foods. However, don't even think about it. Fast foods are incredibly unhealthy and can deter you from your keto journey. Fast foods contain too many harmful chemicals and preservatives; some fast foods don't use real cheese, and their meats sometimes contain hidden sugars among other ingredients.

4. Increase your protein intake:

Protein is an essential and important nutrient necessary for your body. It can soothe your appetite and burn fat more than any other nutrient. Generally, protein is highly effective in weight loss, can increase muscle mass, and may improve your body composition.

5. Increase your sodium intake:

By reducing carbohydrate consumption, your insulin levels fall, which in turn gets rid of extra sodium stored in your body, causing problems such as sodium deficiency. If your body experiences sodium deficiency, you might experience exhaustion, headaches, constipations, etc.
To relieve this problem, increase your sodium intake on a keto diet. Add a teaspoon of salt to daily meals or drink a glass of water with a ¼ teaspoon of salt mixed with it.

6. Be patient:

It is common nature for us to seek immediate gratification. When you start a diet, you may be discouraged to continue if you are not instantly experiencing the benefits immediately. Losing weight and being healthy takes time. In order to attain this goal, allow your body some time to start burning fat instead of glucose. It may take a few days or a couple of weeks, but be patient and don't bail on the diet.

Breakfast Recipes

Breakfast Burrito in a Bowl:

Serves: 4
Total Time: 25 minutes
Macros per serving:
Calories: 613
Protein: 22.9 grams
Fat: 49.9 grams
Carbohydrates: 9.9 grams

What you'll need:

- 6 eggs
- 3 tablespoons of melted butter
- ¼ teaspoon of pepper
- 1 teaspoon of salt
- ½ pound of breakfast sausage, cooked
- ½ cup of sharp cheddar cheese, shredded
- ½ cup of sour cream
- ½ cup of salsa
- ¼ cup of green onion, diced
- 1 avocado, cubed

How to make it:

1. Mix the first four ingredients on the list (eggs, butter, pepper, and salt) in a large bowl.
2. On the instant pot, press sauté. Set the heat to less.
3. Place the egg mixture in the instant pot. Cook for 5-6 minutes, gently stirring using a rubber spatula.
4. When the eggs start to firm, add the cheese and breakfast sausage. Continue cooking until eggs are done. Press Cancel.
5. Divide the mixture into four bowls. Top each bowl with sour cream, salsa green onion, and avocado. Enjoy!

Sausage and Cheddar Frittata:

Serves: 4
Total Time: 45 minutes
Macros per serving:
Calories: 282
Protein: 24 grams
Fat: 12 grams
Carbohydrates: 1 gram

What you'll need:

- ½ cup ground sausage, cooked
- ¼ cup grated cheddar cheese
- 4 eggs
- 2 tablespoons sour cream
- 1 tablespoon butter
- ¼ teaspoon salt
- Pinch of pepper
- 1 ½ cups water

How to make it:

1. Pour the water into your instant pot and lower the rack.
2. Grease a baking dish can fit inside the instant pot with some cooking spray.
3. Whisk along the eggs and cream, in a bowl.
4. Stir in the remaining ingredients.
5. Pour the mixture into the prepared baking dish.
6. Place the dish on the rack and close the lid.
7. Cook on LOW pressure for 17 minutes.
8. Does a quick pressure release?
9. Serve and enjoy!

Herbed Eggs:

Serves: 4
Total Time: 15 minutes
Macros per serving:
Calories: 290
Protein: 16 grams
Fat: 24 grams
Carbohydrates: 4.5 grams

What you'll need:

- 7 eggs
- ¼ - ½ cup milk
- 4 ounces bacon, diced
- 1 teaspoon thyme
- ¼ cup chopped fresh parsley
- 2 tablespoons chopped cilantro
- ½ teaspoon garlic powder
- ¼ teaspoon salt
- 1 ½ cups water

How to make it:

1. Whisk together the eggs, milk, thyme, chopped herbs, salt, and garlic powder.
2. Set the instant pot to SAUTE and place the diced bacon in it.
3. Cook for 2 minutes, or until the bacon becomes crispy.
4. Transfer the bacon to a lubricated baking pan that may work into your instant pot.
5. Pour the egg mixture over.
6. Pour the water into the IP and close the lid.
7. Set the IP to MANUAL and cook on HIGH for 20 minutes.
8. Release the pressure quickly.
9. Serve and enjoy!

Breakfast Bacon Hash:

Serves: 4
Total Time: 40 minutes
Macros per serving:
Calories: 400
Protein: 30.1 grams
Fat: 31.7 grams
Carbohydrates: 13 grams

What you'll need:

- 6 eggs
- 2 red potatoes, diced
- ½ package bacon, chopped
- ½ cup cheddar cheese
- ¼ cup green onions
- ¼ teaspoon black pepper
- ¼ teaspoon salt
- 1 tablespoon milk
- The 6-inch springform pan

How to make it:

1. Add bacon to the instant pot and select the "sauté" function to cook for 3 minutes.
2. Transfer the crispy cooked beacon to the greased "spring pan".
3. Add the potatoes on top of bacon.
4. Crack all the eggs in an exceedingly bowl and whisk them well with the milk.
5. Pour the egg mixture over the top and cover with aluminum foil.
6. Sprinkle salt and pepper on top and cover with aluminum foil.
7. Pour some water into the instant pot, set the trivet inside and place the covered spring pan over the trivet.
8. Press the "manual" key; adjust its setting to high pressure for 20 minutes.
9. After it's done, do a natural unleash to unleash the steam
10. Remove the lid and the spring pan. Transfer the hash to a plate.
11. Sprinkle cheddar cheese on top then serve.

No Fuss Keto Quiche Lorraine:

Serves: 4
Total Time: 55 minutes
Macros per serving:
Calories: 573
Protein: 22 grams
Fat: 53 grams
Carbohydrates: 3 grams

What you'll need:

1. 8 slices of bacon, chopped
2. 4 eggs, large
3. 1 ½ cups of heavy whipping cream
4. ¼ teaspoon of nutmeg
5. ¼ teaspoon of salt
6. Pepper to taste
7. 1 cup of shredded Swiss cheese(approx.. 85 g)
8. 1/3 cup of shredded Swiss cheese (approx.. 25 g) for topping

How to make it:

1. On the instant pot, choose the medium sauté setting. Fry the bacon slices until they are crisp. Set aside.
2. Whisk the eggs, heavy whipping cream, nutmeg, salt and pepper in a mixing bowl.
3. Take a 6-inch cake pan and grease the inside. Add 1 cup of shredded Swiss cheese.
4. Crumble the fried bacon. Sprinkle it on top of the cake pan.
5. Pour the egg mixture into the cake pan.
6. Cover cake pan tender foil (optional).
7. Inside the instant pot, place the steam rack. Add 1 cup of water. Place the cake pan on the steam rack.
8. Select high pressure and set for 25 minutes. Once done, wait another 10 minutes before doing a quick pressure release.
9. Remove the cake pan from the instant pot. Remove the foil.
10. Sprinkle with the remaining shredder Swiss. Remove the foil.
11. Place the pan below a broiler for 5-10 minutes.
12. To serve, use a silicone spatula and run it around the edges of the pan to loosen the quiche. Carefully flip out contents onto a plate. Enjoy!

Pepper Jack and Cheese Egg Muffins:

Serves: 8
Total Time: 25 minutes
Macros per serving:
Calories: 282
Protein: 24 grams
Fat: 12 grams
Carbohydrates: 1 gram

What you'll need:

- ¼ cup shredded pepper jack cheese
- 4 bacon slices
- 4 eggs
- 1 green onion, chopped
- Pinch of garlic powder
- Pinch of pepper
- ¼ teaspoon salt
- 1 ½ cups water

How to make it:

1. Set your instant pot to SAUTE.
2. Cook the bacon for some minutes, till crisp.
3. Wipe off the bacon grease, pour the water inside, and lower the rack.
4. Beat the eggs along with the pepper, garlic powder, and salt.
5. Crumble the bacon and add to this mixture.
6. Stir in the onion and cheese.
7. Pour this mixture into 4 silicone muffin cups.
8. Arrange them on the rack and close the lid.
9. Cook on HIGH for 8 minutes.
10. Wait 2 minutes before releasing the pressure quickly.
11. Serve and enjoy!

Breakfast Bagels:

Serves: 3
Total Time: 30 minutes
Macros per serving:
Calories: 370
Protein: 20 grams
Fat: 30 grams
Carbohydrates: 3.5 grams

What you'll need:

- ¾ cup almond or coconut flour
- 1 ½ cups shredded mozzarella cheese
- 1/8 cup cream cheese
- 1 egg
- 1 teaspoon Xanthan gum
- 1 tablespoon butter, melted
- Pinch of sea salt
- 1 ½ cups water

How to make it:

1. Pour the water into the instant pot and lower the rack.
2. Whisk together the eggs, salt, and xanthan gum.
3. Place the mozzarella in a microwave-safe bowl and microwave until melted.
4. Add the melted cheese to the egg mixture along with the flour.
5. Mix until a ball of dough is formed.
6. Divide the dough into 3 equal pieces.
7. Make three bagels out of the dough and flatten them with your hand.
8. Grease a baking dish with cooking spray and place the bagels on it.
9. Brush the melted butter over them.
10. Place in the IP and close the lid.
11. Choose MANUAL and cook for 15 minutes.
12. Do a quick pressure release.
13. Cut the bagels in half and serve with your favorite toppings.
14. Enjoy!

Black Bean and Egg Casserole:

Serves: 3
Total Time: 35 minutes
Macros per serving:
Calories: 564
Protein: 36.2 grams
Fat: 30.7 grams
Carbohydrates: 23.4 grams

What you'll need:

- 4 large eggs, well-beaten
- ½ lb. mild ground sausage
- ¼ large red onion, chopped
- ½ red bell pepper, chopped
- ½ can black beans, rinsed
- ¼ cup green onions
- ¼ cup flour
- ½ cup cotija cheese*
- ½ cup mozzarella cheese
- Sour cream, cilantro to garnish

How to make it:

1. Add sausage and onion to the instant pot and select the "sauté" function to cook for 3 minutes.
2. Combine flour with eggs and add this mixture to the sausages.
3. Add all the vegetables, cheese, and beans.
4. Secure the lid of the cookware and press the "MANUAL" perform key.
5. Adjust the time to 20 minutes and cook at high pressure.
6. After the beep, unleash the pressure naturally and take away the lid.
7. Remove the inner pot, place a plate on top then flip the pot to transfer the casserole to the plate.
8. Serve warm.

Copy Cat Starbucks Bacon Egg Poppers:

Serves: 9
Total Time: 32 minutes
Macros per serving:
Calories: 124
Protein: 9 grams
Fat: 8 grams
Carbohydrates: 3 grams

What you'll need:

- 4 eggs
- ¼ cup of egg whites
- ¼ cup of heavy whipping cream
- ½ cup of cottage cheese, reduced-fat
- 1 cup of cheese, shredded
- Salt and pepper to taste
- 4 slices of bacon, cooked then crumbled
- ½ green pepper, chopped
- ½ red pepper, chopped
- 1 cup of red onion, chopped
- 1 cup of water

How to make it:

1. Place eggs, egg whites, whipping cream, cottage cheese, shredded cheese, salt, and pepper in a blender. Process for 30-45 seconds or until well-blended.
2. Spoon the mixture into each of the compartments of a silicone baby food container.
3. Sprinkle each compartment with the bacon, peppers, and onions. Cover the container.
4. In the instant pot, place 1 cup of water and the trivet. Place the baby food container on the trivet.
5. Choose the steam setting and cook for 12-15 minutes.
6. Allow natural steam release for 10 minutes.
7. Remove the container from the instant pot and allow to cool.
8. To serve, push the bottom of each container to release the poppers.

Cheesy Chili Mexican Frittata:

Serves: 4

Total Time: 40 minutes

Macros per serving:

Calories: 257

Protein: 14 grams

Fat: 19 grams

Carbohydrates: 5 grams

What you'll need:

- 4 eggs
- 1 cup shredded Mexican blend cheese
- 10 ounces canned green chilies, chopped
- ¼ cup chopped cilantro
- 1 cup half and half
- ½ teaspoon cumin
- ½ teaspoon salt
- ¼ teaspoon pepper
- 2 cups water

How to make it:

1. Pour the water into the IP and lower the rack.
2. Beat together the eggs salt, cumin, half and half, and ½ of the cheese, in a bowl.
3. Stir in the chilies and cilantro.
4. Grease a baking dish with foil and place in the instant pot.
5. Cook for 20 minutes at HIGH.
6. Wait 10 minutes before remaining cheese and cook for 2 more minutes on HIGH, uncovered.
7. Serve and enjoy!

Cheesy Cauliflower Egg Pie:

Serves: 6
Total Time: 30 minutes
Macros per serving:
Calories: 350
Protein: 17 grams
Fat: 25 grams
Carbohydrates: 5.2 grams

What you'll need:

- 8 eggs, whisked
- ½ onion, diced
- 1 teaspoon garlic salt
- 1 teaspoon dried thyme
- 8 ounces grated mozzarella chase
- 2 ounces grated cheddar cheese
- ¼ teaspoon turmeric
- 2 cups cauliflower rice (ground in a food processor)
- ¼ teaspoon pepper
- 1 ½ cups water

How to make it:

1. Pour the water into the instant pot and lower the trivet.
2. Place everything in an exceedingly massive bowl and stir to mix.
3. Grease pie pan with some cooking spray.
4. Pour the cheesy cauliflower mixture into it.
5. Place the pan within the instant pot and shut the lid.
6. Cook on HIGH for 20 minutes.
7. Press CANCEL and wait 5 minutes before doing a quick pressure release.
8. Serve and enjoy!

Korean Steamed Egg:

Serves: 2
Total Time: 10 minutes
Macros per serving:
Calories: 443
Protein: 13.2 grams
Fat: 15.2 grams
Carbohydrates: 12 grams

What you'll need:

- 3 large eggs
- ½ cup cold water
- 3 teaspoons chopped scallions
- Pinch of sesame seeds
- Pinch of garlic powder
- Salt and pepper to taste

How to make it:

1. Add 1 cup water to the instant pot and place the trivet inside.
2. Add all the ingredients in a very bowl and whisk well.
3. Take a heatproof bowl and pour the egg mixture into it.
4. Place the bowl over the trivet.
5. Secure the lid of the cookware and press the "MANUAL" perform key.
6. Adjust the time to five minutes and cook at high.
7. After the beep, unharness the pressure naturally and take away the lid.
8. Serve immediately with rice.

Kale and Egg Shakshuka:

Serves: 4
Total Time: 30 minutes
Macros per serving:
Calories: 123
Protein: 6.8 grams
Fat: 10.2 grams
Carbohydrates: 6.7 grams

What you'll need:

- 1 tablespoon of olive oil
- 2 garlic cloves, minced
- ½ onion, diced
- ½ red bell pepper, diced
- ½ teaspoon of smoked paprika
- 1 teaspoon of chili powder
- ½ teaspoon of cumin, ground
- 2 cups of baby kale
- 1 ½ cups of marinara sauce
- ½ teaspoon of sea salt
- ½ teaspoon of black pepper, ground
- 4 eggs
- 1 tablespoon of fresh parsley, chopped

How to make it:

1. On your instant pot, select the sauté function. Heat the olive oil.
2. Sauté the garlic, onion, red bell pepper, paprika, chili powder, and cumin for 2-3 minutes.
3. Add the baby kale and cook for 2-3 minutes.
4. Add the marinara sauce. Season with salt and pepper.
5. Turn off the pot. Allow cooling 5 minutes.
6. Crack the eggs carefully in the pot, making sure they are evenly spaced.
7. Close and lock the lid and choose low pressure. Set the pot's time for 0 minutes.
8. Quick-release the pressure once the pot beeps.
9. After 2 minutes, unlock and remove the pot's lid.
10. Sprinkle with parsley before serving.

Diced Paprika Eggs:

Serves: 6
Total Time: 15 minutes
Macros per serving:
Calories: 62
Protein: 5 grams
Fat: 4 grams
Carbohydrates: 0 grams

What you'll need:

- ½ teaspoon smoked paprika
- 6 eggs
- ¼ teaspoon salt
- Pinch of pepper
- 1 ½ cups water

How to make it:

1. Pour the water into your instant pot.
2. Crack the eggs into a baking dish, not breaking the yolks.
3. Cover the dish with foil and place on the rack.
4. Close the lid and cook on HIGH for four minutes.
5. Release the pressure quickly and remove the 'loaf' of eggs.
6. Place on a cutting board and dice the eggs finely.
7. Stir in the spices.
8. Serve and enjoy!

Feta and Olive Omelet:

Serves: 2
Total Time: 30 minutes
Macros per serving:
Calories: 300
Protein: 14 grams
Fat: 15 grams
Carbohydrates: 3 grams

What you'll need:

- 6 eggs
- 2 tablespoons milk
- ¼ teaspoon pepper
- ½ teaspoon garlic salt
- A handful of olive slices
- 1 ½ cups water

How to make it:

1. Pour the water into the instant pot and lower the rack.
2. Whisk together the eggs, milk, salt, and pepper.
3. Stir in the diced olives.
4. Grease a baking dish with some cooking spray and pour the egg mixture into it.
5. Place the dish in the IP and close the lid.
6. Cook on HIGH for 15-20 minutes, depending on the desired consistency.
7. Do a quick pressure release.
8. Top the cooked eggs with feta cubes and olives
9. Serve and enjoy!

Chicken Recipe

High Protein Breadless Chicken Sandwich:

Serves: 1
Total Time: 25 minutes
Macros per serving:
Calories: 761
Protein: 52 grams
Fat: 53 grams
Carbohydrates: 5 grams

What you'll need:

- 2 tablespoons of coconut oil, divided
- 6 ounces of chicken breast, boneless, skinless, cut in half lengthwise, and pound with a tenderizer until thin
- ¼ teaspoon of garlic powder
- ¼ teaspoon of salt
- 1/8 teaspoon of pepper
- 1 egg
- ¼ avocado
- 2 tablespoons of homemade mayo
- ¼ cup of white cheddar, shredded

How to make it:

1. Season the pigeon breast with garlic powder, salt, and pepper. Set aside.
2. On the instant pot, select the sauté function. Heat 1 tablespoon of coconut oil. Set the temperature to less. Once hot, fry the egg. Remove the egg from the pot and put aside.
3. Add the remaining coconut oil. Once hot sear the chicken until each side is golden. Select the manual function and set the pot's timer for 8 minutes.
4. While the chicken is cooking, mash the avocado. Once mashed properly, mix in mayo.
5. Once done, does a quick pressure release. Remove the chicken from the pot and pat with a paper towel to get rid of moisture.
6. Place one piece of chicken on a plate, top with an egg, the avocado moisture, shredded cheese, and another piece of chicken. Serve warm.

Soft and Juicy Chicken:

Serves: 10
Total Time: 50 minutes
Macros per serving:
Calories: 270
Protein: 22 grams
Fat: 20 grams
Carbohydrates: 3 grams

What you'll need:

1. 1 3-4 pound chicken
2. 1 tablespoon coconut oil
3. 2 tablespoons lemon juice
4. 2 garlic cloves, peeled
5. 1 teaspoon paprika
6. 1 ½ cups chicken stock
7. ½ teaspoon salt
8. ¼ teaspoon pepper
9. 1 teaspoon onion powder

How to make it:

1. Combine all of the spices in a very tiny bowl.
2. Rub the mixture into the chicken.
3. Melt the coconut oil in your IP on SAUTE.
4. Add the chicken and cook till brunet on all sides.
5. Pour the stock and lemon juice over.
6. Add the garlic cloves.
7. Close and cook on MANUAL for 25 minutes.
8. Let the pressure drop naturally.
9. Serve and enjoy!

Juicy Whole Chicken:

Serves: 10
Total Time: 50 minutes
Macros per serving:
Calories: 270
Protein: 22 grams
Fat: 20 grams
Carbohydrates: 3 grams

What you'll need:

- 1 tablespoon coconut oil
- 1 ½ cups chicken stock
- 2 tablespoons lemon juice
- 2 garlic cloves
- 3-4 pound whole chicken
- ½ teaspoon salt
- ¼ teaspoon black pepper
- 1 teaspoon onion powder

How to make it:

1. Season the chicken with salt, pepper, and onion powder.
2. Melt the coconut oil on SAUTE.
3. Place the chicken in the side in the side and cook on all sides, until golden brown.
4. Pour the stock and the lemon juice inside and add the garlic cloves.
5. Close the lid and set your IP to MANUAL.
6. Cook on HIGH for 25 minutes
7. Release the pressure naturally.
8. Serve and enjoy!

Green Chili Adobo Chicken:

Serves: 6
Total Time: 30 minutes
Macros per serving:
Calories: 204
Protein: 32.9 grams
Fat: 7.2 grams
Carbohydrates: 4.6 grams

What you'll need:

- 6 boneless, skinless chicken breasts
- ½ cup water
- 1 tablespoon turmeric
- 1 tablespoon GOYA adobo all-purpose seasoning with pepper
- Two cups diced tomatoes
- 1 cup diced green chilies

How to make it:

1. Place the chicken breast in the inner pot.
2. Add adobo seasoning pepper to the chicken. Sprinkle on both sides.
3. Add the sliced tomatoes to the chicken.
4. Pour half-cup of water over the chicken.
5. Cover and lock the lid. Use manual setting and set the time to 25 minutes.
6. When cooking is complete at the beep, use 'natural release' to vent the stem for 15 minutes.
7. Use quickly the release option to vent all remaining steam.
8. Remove the pot and shred the chicken inside using two forks.
9. Serve with rice, or fill the tacos with the shredded chicken.

Family-style Crack Chicken:

Serves: 8
Total Time: 30 minutes
Macros per serving:
Calories: 437
Protein: 41 grams
Fat: 28 grams
Carbohydrates: 4 grams

What you'll need:

- 2 slices of bacon, chopped
- 2 pounds of chicken breasts, boneless and skinless
- ½ cup of water
- 2 tablespoons of apple cider vinegar
- 8 ounces of cream cheese
- 1 tablespoon of dried chives
- 1 ½ teaspoon of onion powder
- 1 ½ teaspoon of garlic powder
- 1 teaspoon of red pepper flakes, crushed
- ¼ teaspoon of salt
- ¼ teaspoon of black pepper
- ½ cup of shredded cheddar
- 1 scallion, green and white parts only, thinly sliced

How to make it:

1. One the instant pot, select the sauté function. Wait for about 2 minutes to allow the pot to heat up. Once hot, add the chopped bacon and cook until it becomes crispy. Once done, transfer the bacon to a plate and set aside. Press Cancel on the pot.
2. Place the chicken, water, vinegar, cream cheese, chives, onion powder, garlic powder, red pepper flakes, salt and pepper to the pot. Select manual, high pressure and set the pot's timer for 15 minutes.
3. Once done, do a quick release.
4. Using tongs, transfer the chicken to a separate plate. Shred the chicken and return it back into the pot.
5. Add the cheddar cheese to the pot and stir until well-blended.
6. To serve, sprinkle with the cooked bacon and scallion.

Cheesy Chicken with Jalapenos:

Serves: 4
Total Time: 20 minutes
Macros per serving:
Calories: 310
Protein: 20 grams
Fat: 26 grams
Carbohydrates: 4 grams

What you'll need:

- 1 pound chicken breasts
- 8-ounce cheddar cheese, grated
- ¾ cup sour cream
- 3 jalapenos, seeded and sliced
- ½ cup water
- 8 ounces cream cheese
- Salt and pepper, to taste

How to make it:

1. Whisk together the water, sour cream, and cheeses in the instant pot.
2. Stir in the jalapenos and place the chicken inside.
3. Season with some salt and pepper.
4. Close the lid and cook MANUAL for 12 minutes.
5. Release the pressure quickly.
6. Serve and enjoy!

Hot Taco-Seasoned Chicken:

Serves: 6
Total Time: 35 minutes
Macros per serving:
Calories: 240
Protein: 33 grams
Fat: 9 grams
Carbohydrates: 4.9 grams

What you'll need:

- 1-ounce taco seasoning
- ½ cup red salsa
- ½ cup mild salsa Verde
- 1 ½ pounds chicken breasts, skinless and boneless

How to make it:

1. Place everything in the instant pot.
2. Stir to combine well and close the lid.
3. Set the instant pot to MANUAL.
4. Cook on HIGH for 25 minutes.
5. Does a quick pressure release.
6. With two forks, shred the meat inside the pot.
7. Stir to combine and serve.
8. Enjoy!

Instant Dumplings:

Serves: 4
Total Time: 20 minutes
Macros per serving:
Calories: 610
Protein: 100.5 grams
Fat: 12.1 grams
Carbohydrates: 10 grams

What you'll need:

- 1 cup water
- 2 cups chicken broth
- 1 ½ lb. chicken breast, cubed
- 1 cup chopped carrots
- 1 teaspoon olive oil
- 1 cup frozen peas
- 2 teaspoons oregano
- 1 teaspoon onion powder
- 1 tube (16 oz.) refrigerated biscuits
- 1 teaspoon basil
- ½ teaspoon salt
- 2 cloves minced garlic
- ½ teaspoon pepper

How to make it:

1. Press the biscuits to flatten them, and then cut them into 2-inch strips with a sharp knife.
2. Put the olive oil, onion powder, oregano, chicken, garlic, salt, pepper, and basil into the pot and mix them well.
3. Select the 'sauté' function on your pressure cooker and allow it to cook until the chicken turns brown.
4. Cancel the 'sauté' function when the cooking is finished.
5. Add the water, peas, carrots and chicken broth to the pot. Add the biscuits then stir well.
6. Cover with the lid and lock it.
7. Select the 'MANUAL' function, and set the timer for 5 minutes.
8. After the beep, use the 'natural' release' for 10 minutes to vent all steam.
9. Press 'CANCEL' turn the cooker off and then remove the lid.
10. Serve the cooked chicken in a bowl.

Protein Heavy Creamy Chicken Chili:

Serves: 8
Total Time: 50 minutes
Macros per serving:
Calories: 510
Protein: 41 grams
Fat: 33 grams
Carbohydrates: 9 grams

What you'll need:

- 2 tablespoons of butter
- 1 medium onion, diced
- 10 medium chicken thighs, boneless, skinless, cubed
- 1 pound of frozen cauliflower
- 14 ounce of canned green chilies, diced
- 2 teaspoons of cumin
- 2 teaspoons of oregano
- 2 teaspoons of salt
- 1 teaspoon of black pepper
- 4 cups of chicken broth
- 2 cups of sour cream
- 1 cup of heavy whipping cream

How to make it:

1. On the instant pot, select the sauté setting. Melt the butter on the heated pot.
2. Sauté the onion and chicken and cook until the chicken are golden.
3. Add the cauliflower, chili, cumin, oregano, salt, and pepper. Stir everything together for a few minutes.
4. Add the chicken broth. Seal the pot, select high pressure, and set the pot's timer for 30 minutes.
5. Once done, let the pot sit for 10 minutes before doing a natural pressure release.
6. Once all the pressure has been released, whisk the sour cream and whipping cream in. serve at once.

Salsa Verde Chicken:

Serves: 6
Total Time: 30 minutes
Macros per serving:
Calories: 340
Protein: 55 grams
Fat: 6.8 grams
Carbohydrates: 5 grams

What you'll need:

- 16 ounces salsa Verde
- 2 ½ pounds chicken breasts
- 1 teaspoon cumin
- ¼ teaspoon garlic powder
- 1 teaspoon salt
- ¼ teaspoon pepper
- Pinch of paprika

How to make it:

1. Whisk together the salsa and spices in the instant pot.
2. Add the chicken.
3. Close the IP's lid and choose the MANUAL cooking mode.
4. Cook for 25 minutes on high.
5. Do a quick pressure release.
6. Serve and enjoy!

Barbecue Wings:

Serves: 2
Total Time: 15 minutes
Macros per serving:
Calories: 270
Protein: 35 grams
Fat: 8 grams
Carbohydrates: 3.6 grams

What you'll need:

- 12 chicken wings
- ¼ cup barbecue sauce, sugar-free
- 1 cup of water

How to make it:

1. Pour the water in your instant pot and place the chicken wings inside.
2. Close the lid and cook on HIGH for about 5 minutes.
3. Do a quick pressure release.
4. Rinse the wings and pat them dry with some paper towels.
5. Discard the cooking liquid and place the wings in the IP.
6. Pour the barbecue sauce over and coat them well.
7. Set the IP to SAUTE and cook until sticky on all sides.
8. Serve and enjoy!

Mustard Chicken with Lime Juice:

Serves: 6
Total Time: 35 minutes
Macros per serving:
Calories: 748
Protein: 127.5 grams
Fat: 19.9 grams
Carbohydrates: 4.3 grams

What you'll need:

- 2 tablespoons olive oil
- ¼ cup lemon juice
- ¾ cup chicken broth
- 2 lbs. chicken thighs, boneless
- 2 tablespoons Italian seasoning
- 3 lbs. red potatoes, quartered
- 3 tablespoons Dijon mustard
- Salt and pepper

How to make it:

1. Place the oil and the chicken in the instant pot. Sprinkle salt and pepper to taste.
2. In a separate bowl, combine the lemon juice, the chicken broth, and the Dijon mustard, and mix them well.
3. Now add the potatoes, cut into 4 pieces, along with the remaining seasoning.
4. Secure the lid and select the 'MANUAL' option-15 minutes at high pressure.
5. Let it cook until the beep. Release the steam over 15 minutes using the 'natural' release' method.
6. Serve.

Hassle-Free Turmeric Chicken:

Serves: 6
Total Time: 60 minutes
Macros per serving:
Calories: 404
Protein: 47 grams
Fat: 21 grams
Carbohydrates: 3 grams

What you'll need:

- 4 chicken breast, boneless and skinless
- 10 cloves of garlic, peeled and diced
- ¼ cup of turmeric ghee(or ¼ cup regular ghee with 1 teaspoon of pure turmeric powder)
- 1 teaspoon of salt

How to make it:

1. Place all the ingredients in the instant pot.
2. Select high pressure and set the pot's timer for 35 minutes.
3. Once done, do a natural pressure release for 10 to 15 minutes. Afterward, do a quick release to get rid of any remaining pressure.
4. Shred the chicken breast in the pot.
5. Serve with cauliflower rice for a side of vegetables. Bon appetite!

Cream Cheese Chicken with Bacon:

Serves: 4
Total Time: 40 minutes
Macros per serving:
Calories: 620
Protein: 48 grams
Fat: 38 grams
Carbohydrates: 6 grams

What you'll need:

- 8-ounce cream cheese
- 8 bacon slices, cooked and crumbled
- 2 pounds chicken breasts
- 1 packet ranch seasoning
- 4 ounces cheddar cheese, shredded
- 2 tablespoons arrowroot
- 1 cup water

How to make it:

1. Whisk together the cream cheese, water, and seasoning, in the IP.
2. Add the chicken breast inside.
3. Close the lid and cook on HIGH for twenty five minutes.
4. Press CANCEL, do a quick pressure release and transfer the chicken to a cutting board.
5. Shred with two forks.
6. Set your IP to SAUTE and stir in the arrowroot,
7. Add shredded chicken, bacon, and cheddar, and cook for 3-4 minutes, or until thickened.
8. Serve and enjoy!

Spinach Duck Breast:

Serves: 6
Total Time: 40 minutes
Macros per serving:
Calories: 455
Protein: 45 grams
Fat: 26 grams
Carbohydrates: 1 gram

What you'll need:

- 2 pounds duck breasts, skinless and boneless
- 1 cup chopped spinach, packed
- ½ cup chicken stock
- 1 teaspoon oregano
- ¾ cup heavy cream
- 1 teaspoon onion powder
- ½ cup chopped sun-dried tomatoes
- ½ cup grated parmesan cheese

How to make it:

1. Combine the garlic, onion powder, oil, and oregano, and rub the mixture into the meat.
2. Set your IP to SAUTE and cook the duck until golden on all sides.
3. Pour the stock over, close the lid, and cook on high for 5 minutes.
4. Press CANCEL and release the pressure quickly.
5. Stir in the spinach, tomatoes, and heavy cream.
6. Close the lid and cook on HIGH for another 5 minutes.
7. Do a quick pressure release again serve and enjoy!

Red Meat Recipes

Mack Mongolian Beef and Broccoli Stir Fry:

Serves: 6
Total Time: 40 minutes
Macros per serving:
Calories: 310
Protein: 41 grams
Fat: 19 grams
Carbohydrates: 10 grams

What you'll need:

- 1 tablespoon of canola oil
- 4 cloves of garlic, minced
- 1 ½ pound of boneless chuck roast beef, sliced into thin strips
- ½ cup of broth beef broth
- ¼ cup of low-carb sweetener of your choice
- ½ cup of low-sodium soy sauce
- 12 ounces of broccoli florets
- 1 tablespoon of corn starch

How to make it:

1. On the instant pot, select the sauté function. Heat the canola oil. Once hot, add the garlic and beef. Cook until browned. Stir frequently.
2. Add the beef broth, sweetener, and soy sauce in the pot. Stir well. Turn off the sauté mode, seal the lid, and cook at High pressure for 15 minutes.
3. Meanwhile, microwave the broccoli 3-4 minutes.
4. Once the pot is done, do a manual pressure release. Uncover the pot.
5. Remove a quarter cup of liquid from the pot and mix it with corn starch in a separate bowl. Once smooth, place it back in the pot.
6. Select sauté mode and medium heat. Simmer for 5 minutes to thicken the sauce. Stir frequently. Turn the pot off.
7. Add the broccoli into the pot. Stir to coat the broccoli with the sauce.
8. Serve at once with a side of vegetables or cauliflower rice.

Herb-Packed Meatloaf:

Serves: 6
Total Time: 55 minutes
Macros per serving:
Calories: 280
Protein: 25 grams
Fat: 13.8 grams
Carbohydrates: 1.5 grams

What you'll need:

- 1 teaspoon rosemary
- 2 teaspoons thyme
- 1 teaspoon oregano
- 1 ½ teaspoons parsley
- ½ teaspoon sage
- 1 teaspoon garlic salt
- ¼ teaspoon pepper
- 2 pounds ground beef
- 3 tablespoons olive oil
- 2 eggs
- 1 ½ cup water

How to make it:

1. Pour the water into the IP. Lower the trivet.
2. Grease a loaf pan with the olive oil.
3. Place all of the ingredients in a bowl and mix with your hand to combine well.
4. Press the mixture into the pan.
5. Place the loaf pan inside the instant pot and close the lid.
6. Choose MANUAL and cook on high for 30-35 minutes.
7. Release the pressure for 10 minutes.
8. Serve and enjoy!

Instant Fall-Apart Beef Roast:

Serves: 4
Total Time: 80 minutes
Macros per serving:
Calories: 750
Protein: 60 grams
Fat: 50 grams
Carbohydrates: 2.5 grams

What you'll need:

- 1 onion, sliced
- 2 pounds beef roast
- 2 cups beef broth
- 2 tablespoons coconut oil
- Salt and pepper, to taste

How to make it:

1. Melt the coconut oil in your instant pot on SAUTE.
2. Meanwhile, season the beef with some salt and pepper.
3. Place the meat inside the IP and sear on all sides until browned.
4. Place the onion slices on top and pour the beef broth over.
5. Close the lid and cook on MANUAL for 70 minutes.
6. Do a quick pressure release.
7. Serve and enjoy!

Gingery Beef Broccoli:

Serves: 4
Total Time: 50 minutes
Macros per serving:
Calories: 270
Protein: 25 grams
Fat: 12 grams
Carbohydrates: 7 grams

What you'll need:

- 1 pound beef, chopped
- 1 teaspoon minced garlic
- 1 ½ teaspoons grated ginger
- 1 onion, quartered
- ¼ cup coconut aminos
- 12 ounces broccoli florets, frozen
- 2 tablespoons fish sauce
- Salt and pepper, to taste

How to make it:

1. Place everything but the broccoli, in your instant pot.
2. Stir until combined and close the lid.
3. Cook on MANUAL/STEW at the default set time.
4. When the timer goes off, release the pressure quickly.
5. Stir in the broccoli.
6. Cook on SAUTE with the lid off for 5 minutes.
7. Serve immediately.
8. Enjoy!

Better-Than-Chipotle Barbacoa Beef:

Serves: 9
Total Time: 85 minutes
Macros per serving:
Calories: 153
Protein: 24 grams
Fat: 12 grams
Carbohydrates: 2 grams

What you'll need:

- 1 cup water
- Juice of 1 lime
- 5 cloves of garlic
- ½ medium onion
- 2-4 tablespoons of chipotles in adobo sauce
- 1 tablespoon of ground cumin
- 1 tablespoon of ground oregano
- ½ teaspoon of ground cloves
- 3 pounds of beef eye of round or bottom round roast, all fat trimmed, cut into 3-inch pieces
- 2 ½ teaspoons of kosher salt
- Black pepper
- 1 teaspoon of oil
- 3 bay leaves

How to make it:

1. Place water, lime juice, garlic, onion, chipotles, cumin, oregano, cloves in a blender. Puree until you get a smooth consistency. Set aside.
2. Season the beef with salt and black pepper. On the instant pot, select sauté. Heat the oil. Once hot, cook the meat until brown on all sides.
3. Add the pureed sauce and bay leaves. Cover the pot. Cook on high pressure for 65 minutes.
4. Check the meat for tenderness. Once cooked and tender, remove the meat and transfer it into a dish. Discard the bay leaf. Save the liquid for later
5. Shred the meat and place it back into the pot. Add salt and cumin, to taste. Add 1 ½ cups of the saved liquid.
6. Stir. Serve with cauli-rice or a side of vegetable.

Cream Garlic Pork Sausage:

Serves: 4
Total Time: 35 minutes
Macros per serving:
Calories: 410
Protein: 25 grams
Fat: 30 grams
Carbohydrates: 5 grams

What you'll need:

- 1 pound pork sausage
- ¼ cup arrowroot
- 4 garlic cloves, minced
- 2 cups milk
- 1 teaspoon thyme
- ¼ teaspoon pepper
- ½ tablespoon olive oil
- ½ teaspoon salt

How to make it:

1. Heat the oil your IP on SAUTE.
2. Added the garlic and thyme then cook for one minute.
3. Add sausage and cook it until it becomes brown. Make sure to break the sausage as cooking.
4. Pour 1 ½ cups of the milk over it.
5. Close and cook on HIGH for 5 minutes.
6. Meanwhile, whisk together the arrowroot, remaining milk, salt, and pepper.
7. Do a quick pressure release and whisk in the arrowroot mixture.
8. Set the IP to SAUTE and cook for 5 minutes, or until thickened.
9. Serve and enjoy!

Creamy Mushroom Pork Chops:

Serves: 4
Total Time: 35 minutes
Macros per serving:
Calories: 380
Protein: 20 grams
Fat: 30 grams
Carbohydrates: 1 gram

What you'll need:

- 1 can of cream of mushroom soup
- 2 tablespoons olive oil
- 4 pork chops
- ¼ teaspoon pepper
- 1 ½ cups water

How to make it:

1. Heat the oil in your instant pot on SAUTE.
2. Season the pork chops with some pepper and cook them until browned on all sides. Transfer to a plate.
3. Whisk together the water and cream of mushroom soup in the pot.
4. Return the pork chops and close the lid.
5. Cook on HIGH for 18 minutes.
6. Let the pressure drop naturally, about 10 minutes.
7. Serve and enjoy!

Beef and Pork Gumbo:

Serves: 3
Total Time: 4 hours 40 minutes
Macros per serving:
Calories: 181
Protein: 20.4 grams
Fat: 8.5 grams
Carbohydrates: 4.8 grams

What you'll need:

- ¼ tablespoon olive oil
- ¼ lbs. grass-fed ground beef
- ¼ lbs. ground pork
- 1 medium tomatillo, chopped
- 1/8 small yellow onion, chopped
- ½ jalapeno pepper, chopped
- ½ garlic clove, minced
- ¼ (6oz) can sugar-free tomato sauce
- ¼ tablespoon chili powder
- ¼ tablespoon ground cumin
- Salt and freshly ground black pepper to taste.
- 1 tablespoon water
- 2 tablespoons cheddar cheese, shredded

How to make it:

1. Put the oil and all ingredients into the instant pot.
2. Stir well and secure the lid.
3. Set the cooker to 'slow cook' at high heat for 4 hours.
4. 'Natural release' the steam and remove the lid.
5. Serve hot.

Sugar and Spice Asian Pulled Pork:

Serves: 6
Total Time: 2 hours
Macros per serving:
Calories: 125
Protein: 22 grams
Fat: 5 grams
Carbohydrates: 3 grams

What you'll need:

- 1 cup of pork bone broth
- 4 pounds of pork roast, excess fat trimmed
- 2 to 3 tablespoons of lard or tallow
- ¼ cup coconut sugar
- ½ cup of coconut aminos
- 6 cloves of garlic, minced
- 1 tablespoon of Chinese five-spice
- 1 teaspoon of turmeric
- 1 ½ teaspoon of dried ginger
- 2 tablespoons of rice wine vinegar
- Juice and zest of 1 lime
- 1 teaspoon of Sriracha sauce

How to make it:

1. On the instant pot, select the sauté function. Begin warming up the pot.
2. Add the bone broth and the pork roast into the pot.
3. Whisk in all the remaining ingredients in a separate bowl. Pour the mixture over the pork roast.
4. Seal the lid and the vent. Press Keep warm/cancel.
5. Cook on manual for 90 minutes.
6. Once done, do a natural pressure release for 20 minutes. When done, quick release all remaining pressure. Remove the lid.
7. Shred the pork.
8. Press sauté on the pot. Bring the sauce to a simmer. Simmer for until the sauce has thickened.
9. Return the shredded pork to the pot. Stir well to coat it in the sauce.
10. Serve over cauli-rice, zoodles, stir-fried veggies, and as a filling for tacos.

Spicy and Smokey Pork:

Serves: 4
Total Time: 75 minutes
Macros per serving:
Calories: 760
Protein: 75 grams
Fat: 40 grams
Carbohydrates: 2.2 grams

What you'll need:

- ½ teaspoon chili powder
- 1 teaspoon cumin
- 1 teaspoon thyme
- 1 teaspoon oregano
- 1 teaspoon smoked paprika
- 1 teaspoon sweetener
- 1 tablespoon coconut oil
- 1 teaspoon ground ginger
- ½ teaspoon onion powder
- 1 teaspoon garlic powder
- 2 pounds pork roast
- ½ teaspoon pepper
- 1 ½ cups beef broth

How to make it:

1. Melt the coconut oil in your IP on SAUTE.
2. Combine all of the herbs and spices and rub the mixture into the pork.
3. Place the pork in the IP and sear on all sides, until browned.
4. Combine the liquid smoke with the broth and pour over.
5. Close the lid and cook for 45 minutes on HIGH.
6. Release the pressure naturally.
7. Serve and enjoy!

Braised Lamb Shanks:

Serves: 4
Total Time: 50 minutes
Macros per serving:
Calories: 590
Protein: 53 grams
Fat: 40 grams
Carbohydrates: 7.2 grams

What you'll need:

- 4 lamb shanks
- 3 tablespoons almond flour
- ½ yellow bell pepper, diced
- 8 ounces canned diced tomatoes
- ½ onion, diced
- 2 tablespoons olive oil
- 1 teaspoon minced garlic
- 2/3 cup beef broth

How to make it:

1. Place the lambs and flour in a plastic bag and shake to coat well.
2. Heat half of the oil in your IP on SAUTE.
3. Add the lamb and cook till suntanned on all sides. Transfer to a plate.
4. Heat the remaining oil and cook the onions and pepper for 3 minutes.
5. Add garlic and cook for another minute.
6. Stir in the tomatoes and cook for 3 more minutes.
7. Pour in the broth over and stir to combine.
8. Return the shanks to the pot.
9. Close the lid and cook on HIGH for twenty five minutes.
10. Let the pressure drop naturally.
11. Serve the lamb drizzled with some of the cooking sauce.
12. Serve and enjoy!

Greek Style Lamb:

Serves: 2
Total Time: 70 minutes
Macros per serving:
Calories: 664
Protein: 56.9 grams
Fat: 44.8 grams
Carbohydrates: 4.8 grams

What you'll need:

- 1 lb. lamb meat, ground
- 4 garlic cloves
- 1 teaspoon rosemary
- ¾ teaspoon salt
- ¼ teaspoon black pepper
- ½ small onion, chopped
- 1 teaspoon dried oregano
- 1 teaspoon ground marjoram
- ¾ cup water

How to make it:

1. Chop the garlic, onions, rosemary, and marjoram in a food processor.
2. Add the ground beef and the salt and pepper to the mixture and combine well.
3. Compress the beef mixture to make compact 'loaf'.
4. Cover it tightly with foil and make some holes in it.
5. Pour water into the instant pot and place the trivet inside.
6. Place the loaf pan over the trivet and secure the lid.
7. Cook on 'MANUAL' at air mass for quarter-hour.
8. 'Quick release' the steam, then remove the lid.
9. Serve warm.

Thanksgiving Leg of Lamb:

Serves: 8
Total Time: 45minutes
Macros per serving:
Calories: 432
Protein: 45 grams
Fat: 26 grams
Carbohydrates: 1 gram

What you'll need:

- 2 tablespoons of avocado oil, divided
- 3-4 pounds of boneless leg of lamb
- Salt and pepper (to taste)
- 2 tablespoons of fresh rosemary, chopped
- 4 cloves of garlic, crushed
- 2 cups of water

How to make it:

1. Using paper towels, pat the lamb dry. Season with salt and pepper. Cover evenly.
2. On the instant pot, select sauté. Heat the oil. Once hot, cook the lamb until brown.
3. Once the lamb is evenly browned on all sides, remove the lamb from the pot. Sprinkle the lamb from the pot. Sprinkle the lamb with rosemary and garlic.
4. Place the rack in the pot and pour water into the pot.
5. Place the lamb on the rack. Select the meat/stew function. Cook for 30 to 35 minutes.
6. Once done, do a natural pressure release.
7. Preheat the broiler. Broil the lamb for 2 minutes. Note: you can skip this step if desired. Otherwise, remove the lamb from the pot and let it sit for 10 minutes before slicing.

Sage and Marjoram Lamb:

Serves: 4
Total Time: 80 minutes
Macros per serving:
Calories: 620
Protein: 58 grams
Fat: 26 grams
Carbohydrates: 3 grams

What you'll need:

- 1 ½ teaspoon sage
- 1 ½ teaspoons marjoram
- ¼ teaspoon thyme
- 1 bay leaf
- 2 teaspoons minced garlic
- 2 tablespoons arrowroot
- 1 ½ cups chicken broth
- 6 pounds leg of lamb
- Salt and pepper, to taste

How to make it:

1. Heat the oil in your IP on SAUTE.
2. Combine the herbs with garlic and salt and pepper, and rub into the meat.
3. Place the lamb in the IP and sear on all sides, until browned.
4. Pour the broth over and add the bay leaf.
5. Close the lid and cook for 60 minutes on MEAT/STEW.
6. Release the pressure quickly and transfer the lamb to a plate.
7. Set the IP to SATE and whisk in the arrowroot.
8. Cook until the sauce is thickened.
9. Drizzle over the lamb.
10. Serve and enjoy!

Port and Garlic Lamb:

Serves: 4
Total Time: 30 minutes
Macros per serving:
Calories: 610
Protein: 55 grams
Fat: 35 grams
Carbohydrates: 8.2 grams

What you'll need:

- 1 tablespoon olive oil
- 2 pounds lamb shanks
- 1 tablespoon tomato paste
- 10 whole garlic cloves
- 1 teaspoon balsamic vinegar
- ½ cup port wine
- 1 teaspoon rosemary
- 1 tablespoon butter
- ½ cup chicken broth

How to make it:

1. Heat the oil in your instant pot on SAUTE.
2. Place the lamb shanks in the pot and cook until browned on all sides.
3. Add the remaining ingredients, except for the vinegar and butter.
4. Close the lid and set to MANUAL.
5. Cook on HIGH for about 20 minutes.
6. Let the pressure come down naturally.
7. Stir in the butter and vinegar just before serving.
8. Enjoy!

Seafood Recipes

Broccoli and Shrimp Stir Fry:

Serves: 4

Total Time: 20 minutes

Macros per serving:

Calories: 173

Protein: 19.4 grams

Fat: 13 grams

Carbohydrates: 5.8 grams

What you'll need:

- 2 tablespoons of coconut oil
- 1 pound of medium shrimp, shelled and deveined
- 2 cups of broccoli florets
- ½ cup of zucchini, diced
- ½ cup of button mushrooms
- 2 cloves of garlic
- 1/8 teaspoons of red pepper flakes
- ¼ cup of soy sauce
- 2 cups of cooked cauliflower rice

How to make it:

1. On the instant pot, press sauté. Heat the coconut oil. Cook the shrimp for 5 minutes. Remove the shrimp and set aside.
2. Place the broccoli, zucchini, mushrooms, garlic, red pepper flakes, and soy sauce. Stir-fry for 5 minutes.
3. Add shrimp back to the pot. Press Cancel on the pot.
4. Scoop some warmed cauliflower rice into serving bowls and top with the shrimp-vegetable stir-fry. Serve warm.

Fish Stock:

Serves: 6
Total Time: 65 minutes
Macros per serving:
Calories: 42
Protein: 5.6 grams
Fat: 2 grams
Carbohydrates: 0 grams

What you'll need:

- 1 cup chopped celery
- 1 tablespoon olive oil
- 1 teaspoon minced garlic
- 2 lemongrass stalks, chopped
- 1 cup chopped carrots
- A handful of thyme
- 2 salmon heads, quartered

How to make it:

1. Heat the oil in your IP on SAUTE.
2. Add salmon heads and cook for 2 minutes.
3. Add the remaining ingredients.
4. Pour water until the IP reaches 3 quarts.
5. Close the lid and choose SOUP.
6. Cook for 45 minutes.
7. Release the pressure for 15 minutes.
8. Strain and store.
9. Enjoy!

Seafood Paella:

Serves: 4
Total Time: 17 minutes
Macros per serving:
Calories: 155
Protein: 7 grams
Fat: 5 grams
Carbohydrates: 6.8 grams

What you'll need:

- 2 cups mussels
- 2 cups ground cauliflower
- 2 cup fish stock
- 1 cup scallops
- 2 bell peppers, diced
- 1 tablespoon coconut oil
- Pinch of saffron
- ½ onion dived

How to make it:

1. Melt the coconut oil in the instant pot.
2. Add onion and peppers and cook for 3-4 minutes.
3. Add the saffron and scallops and continue cooking for 2 more minutes.
4. Stir in the fish stick, mussels, and cauliflower.
5. Close the lid and choose MANUAL.
6. Cook on HIGH for 6 minutes.
7. Do a quick pressure release.
8. Serve and enjoy!

Super-Easy Salmon Fillets:

Serves: 3
Total Time: 13 minutes
Macros per serving:
Calories: 63
Protein: 9.2 grams
Fat: 2.9 grams
Carbohydrates: 0.2 grams

What you'll need:

- 1 cup water
- 3 lemon slices
- 1(5-oz.) salmon fillet
- 1 teaspoon fresh lemon juice
- Salt and ground black pepper, to taste
- Fresh cilantro (garnish)

How to make it:

1. Add the water to the instant pot and place trivet inside.
2. In a shallow bowl, place the salmon fillet. Sprinkle salt and pepper over it.
3. Squeeze some lemon juice on top then place a lemon slice over the salmon fillet.
4. Cover the lid and lock it. Set its pressure release handle to "sealing" position.
5. Use "steam" function on your cooker for 3 minutes to cook.
6. After the beep, do a quick release and release the steam.
7. Remove the lid, and then serve with the lemon slice and fresh cilantro on top.

Keto Shrimp Paella:

Serves: 4
Total Time: 25 minutes
Macros per serving:
Calories: 344
Protein: 38 grams
Fat: 17 grams
Carbohydrates: 8 grams

What you'll need:

- 4 tablespoons of butter
- 1 onion, chopped
- 4 cloves of garlic, chopped
- 1 pound of jumbo shrimp, shell, and tail on
- ¼ teaspoon of black pepper
- 1 teaspoon of paprika
- ¼ teaspoon of red pepper flakes
- 1 pinch of saffron threads
- ½ teaspoon of salt
- 1 teaspoon of turmeric
- 1 red pepper, chopped
- 1 cup of cauli-rice
- 1 cup of chicken broth
- ½ cup of white wine
- Optional: ¼ cup of cilantro

How to make it:

1. On the instant pot, select sauté. Melt the butter and add the onions. When the onions have softened, add garlic.
2. Add black pepper, paprika, red pepper flakes, saffron threads, salt, and turmeric. Stir everything together for a minute. Add the red peppers.
3. Add the rice and stir. Cook for a minute. Add the chicken broth and white wine. Make sure the rice is covered.
4. Once cooked, add the shrimp on top of the cooked rice. Turn the pot off, cover, but make sure the valve is set to sealing.
5. Set the pot to manual and cook for minutes
6. Once done, do a quick pressure release.
7. Serve with cilantro.

White Fish Stew:

Serves: 6
Total Time: 20 minutes
Macros per serving:
Calories: 165
Protein: 24 grams
Fat: 13 grams
Carbohydrates: 5 grams

What you'll need:

- 1 onion, diced
- 1 carrot, sliced
- 2 celery stalks, diced
- 1 cup heavy cream
- 1 pound white fish fillets
- 3 cups fish broth
- 1 cup chopped broccoli
- 1 cup chopped cauliflower
- 1 cup chopped kale
- 2 tablespoons butter
- Salt and pepper, to taste

How to make it:

1. Melt the butter in your instant pot on SAUTE.
2. Sauté the onions for 3 minutes.
3. Stir all of the ingredients, except for the cream.
4. Close the lid and select MANUAL.
5. Cook on HIGH for 5 minutes.
6. Do a natural pressure release.
7. Stir in the heavy cream.
8. Discard the bay leaf and serve.
9. Enjoy!

Almond Tilapia:

Serves: 4
Total Time: 10 minutes
Macros per serving:
Calories: 326
Protein: 44 grams
Fat: 15 grams
Carbohydrates: 1.3 grams

What you'll need:

- 4 tilapia fillets
- 1 teaspoon olive oil
- 2 tablespoons Dijon mustard
- 2/3 cup sliced almonds
- ¼ teaspoon lemon pepper
- 1 cup water

How to make it:

1. Pour the water into your instant pot and lower the rack.
2. Whisk together the oil, mustard, and pepper.
3. Brush the almond fillets with the mixture.
4. Coat the tilapia in sliced almonds.
5. Arrange on the rack of the instant pot.
6. Close the lid and cook for five minutes on HIGH.
7. Do a quick pressure release.
8. Serve and enjoy!

Lime-filled Salmon Fillet:

Serves: 2
Total Time: 25 minutes
Macros per serving:
Calories: 192
Protein: 23.3 grams
Fat: 10.9 grams
Carbohydrates: 0.7 grams

What you'll need:

- 2 (4 oz.) salmon fillets
- ½ tablespoon olive oil
- ½ teaspoon garlic, minced
- ½ cup homemade chicken broth
- ½ teaspoon lemon zest (freshly grated)
- 1 tablespoon fresh lemon juice
- Salt and black pepper, to taste

How to make it:

1. Put all the ingredients into the instant pot and mix them well.
2. Secure the lid and switch its pressure unleash handle to "sealing" position.
3. Select the "MANUAL" operate at high for five minutes.
4. After the beep, release the steam naturally for 10 minutes.
5. Remove the lid and dish out the salmon fillets beside their sauce.
6. Serve.

Quick Salmon:

Serves: 4
Total Time: 20 minutes
Macros per serving:
Calories: 382
Protein: 41 grams
Fat: 15 grams
Carbohydrates: 4 grams

What you'll need:

- 3 medium lemons
- ¾ cup water
- 4 salmon fillets
- 1 bunch of fresh dill weed
- 1 tablespoon of unsalted butter
- ¼ teaspoon of salt
- ¼ teaspoon of black pepper, ground

How to make it:

1. Mix ¼ cup of fresh lemon juice and ¾ cup of water in the instant pot. Place the metal steamer insert in the pot.
2. Place the salmon on the steamer insert.
3. Top the salmon with fresh dill and a slice of fresh lemon.
4. Lock the lid and cook on manual for 5 minutes.
5. Once done, press Cancel. Quickly release the pressure.
6. Serve at once with butter, salt and pepper, and extra dill and lemon.

Haddock and Cheddar:

Serves: 4
Total Time: 30 minutes
Macros per serving:
Calories: 195
Protein: 18 grams
Fat: 18 grams
Carbohydrates: 5.5 grams

What you'll need:

- 12-ounce haddock fillets
- 1 tablespoon butter
- ½ cup heavy cream
- 5-ounce cheddar cheese, grated
- 3 tablespoons diced onions
- ¼ teaspoon garlic salt
- ¼ teaspoon pepper

How to make it:

1. Melt the butter within the instant pot on SAUTE.
2. Sauté the onions for 2 minutes.
3. Season the fish with salt and pepper.
4. Place in the IP and cook for 2 minutes per side.
5. Pour the cream over and top with the cheese.
6. Cook on MANUAL for 5 minutes.
7. Do a natural pressure release.
8. Serve and enjoy!

Lemon Pepper Salmon:

Serves: 4
Cooking time: 10 minutes
Macros per serving:
Calories: 180
Protein: 25 grams
Fat: 8 grams
Carbohydrates: 1.5 grams

What you'll need:

- 4 salmon fillets
- 1 ½ cups water
- 1 teaspoon lemon pepper
- Juice from 1 lemon
- 8 lemon slices

How to make it:

1. Pour the water into the instant pot. Lower the rack.
2. Season the salmon with the lemon pepper.
3. Arrange it on the rack, drizzle with lemon juice, and place lemon slices on top.
4. Close the lid and choose MANUAL.
5. Cook on HIGH for 4 minutes.
6. Serve and enjoy!

Spicy Salmon Meal:

Serves: 4
Total Time: 12 minutes
Macros per serving:
Calories: 159
Protein: 22.4 grams
Fat: 7.4 grams
Carbohydrates: 1.5 grams

What you'll need:

- 2 cups water
- 2 garlic cloves. Minced
- 2 teaspoons powdered stevia
- 2 tablespoons red chili powder
- 2 teaspoon ground cumin
- Salt and freshly grated black pepper, to taste
- 2 lbs. salmon fillet, cut into 8 pieces

How to make it:

1. Pour 2 cups of water within the insert of the moment pot. Set the trivet in it.
2. In a separate bowl, add all the ingredients and blend well.
3. Pour this mixture over the salmon fillets and rub it everywhere it.
4. Place the salmon slices over the trivet in a very single layer.
5. Top each fillet with a lemon slice.
6. Secure the lid and choose "steam" perform for two minutes.
7. After the beep, do a fast unharness so take away the lid.
8. Serve immediately.

Teriyaki Glazed Sea Scallops:

Serves: 6
Total Time: 30 minutes
Macros per serving:
Calories: 270
Protein: 31 grams
Fat: 6 grams
Carbohydrates: 24 grams

What you'll need:

- 1 tablespoon of avocado oil
- 1 pound of jumbo sea scallops
- 3 tablespoons of sugar-free maple syrup
- ½ cup of coconut aminos
- ½ teaspoon of sea salt
- ½ teaspoon of ground ginger
- ½ teaspoon of garlic powder
- To garnish: fresh minced chives

How to make it:

1. On the instant pot, select sauté. Heat the oil and sear the scallops for a minute on each side.
2. Whisk all remaining ingredients, except for the chives.
3. Pour the whisked sauce into the pot, over the scallops.
4. Seal the lid. Press the warm/cancel button. Secure the pressure valve and select the steam button. Cook for 2 minutes.
5. Once done, quick release the pressure.
6. Remove the scallops. Set aside. Allow the sauce to thicken by pressing sauté.
7. Garnished with minced chives before serving.

Lime and Garlic Flavored Octopus:

Serves: 4
Total Time: 20 minutes
Macros per serving:
Calories: 120
Protein: 0 grams
Fat: 3 grams
Carbohydrates: 1.5 grams

What you'll need:

- 1 teaspoon chopped cilantro
- 2 tablespoons olive oil
- 10 ounces octopus
- 2 teaspoons garlic powder
- 3 tablespoons lime juice
- Salt and pepper, to taste

How to make it:

1. Place the octopus in the steaming basket.
2. Season with garlic powder, salt, and pepper.
3. Drizzle with olive and lime juice.
4. Pour the water into the IP and lower the steaming basket.
5. Close the lid and cook for 8 minutes on HIGH.
6. Does a quick pressure release.
7. Serve and enjoy!

Simple Lobster Tails:

Serves: 4
Total Time: 25 minutes
Macros per serving:
Calories: 190
Protein: 19 grams
Fat: 12 grams
Carbohydrates: 0 grams

What you'll need:

- 4 lobster tails
- 1 cup water
- ½ cup white wine
- ½ cup butter, melted

How to make it:

1. Pour the water and the white wine in the instant pot. Lower the steaming basket.
2. Cut the lobster tails in half and place them in the basket.
3. Close the lid and choose MANUAL.
4. Cook on LOW for 5 minutes.
5. Does a natural pressure release.
6. Place on a platter and drizzle with melted butter.
7. Serve and enjoy!

Vegetable Recipes

Sweet and Zesty Brussels sprouts:

Serves: 8
Total Time: 15 minutes
Macros per serving:
Calories: 65
Protein: 3 grams
Fat: 5 grams
Carbohydrates: 6 grams

What you'll need:

- 1 teaspoon of salt
- ¼ teaspoon of black pepper
- 2 tablespoons of sugar-free maple syrup
- 1 tablespoon of buttery spread
- 1 teaspoon of orange zest, grated
- ¼ cup of orange juice, freshly squeezed
- 2 pounds of Brussels sprouts, trimmed and rinsed with cold water

How to make it:

1. Place all ingredients into the instant pot. Seal the lid and make sure a quick release switch is closed.
2. Cook on manual for 3 to 4 minutes. Once done turn off the pot and do a quick pressure release.
3. Stir well so that sauce covers all the Brussels sprouts.

Southern Collard Greens:

Serves: 5
Total Time: 23 minutes
Macros per serving:
Calories: 106
Protein: 4.3 grams
Fat: 6.9 grams
Carbohydrates: 2.3 grams

What you'll need:

- 2 bunches collard greens
- 2 tablespoons olive oil
- 1 cut into thin rings small yellow onion
- 3 minced garlic cloves
- Pinch of red pepper flakes
- 1 cup water
- Salt, to taste

How to make it:

1. Remove the tough stems of collard greens and then, cut into thin strands.
2. Place the oil within the instant pot and choose "sauté". Then add the onion and cook for about 4-5 minutes.
3. Add the garlic and red pepper flakes and cook for regarding one minute.
4. Select the "CANCEL" and stir in collard greens and water.
5. Secure the lid and place the pressure Valve to "seal" position.
6. Select "MANUAL" and cook below "High Pressure" for regarding three minutes.
7. Select the "CANCEL" and punctiliously do a fast unleash.
8. Remove the lid and stir in salt.
9. Serve hot.

Fake Wild Mushroom Risotto:

Serves: 4
Total Time: 10 minutes
Macros per serving:
Calories: 110
Protein: 2.5 grams
Fat: 12 grams
Carbohydrates: 6 grams

What you'll need:

- 1 large cauliflower head, riced
- 1 cups veggie broth
- ½ onion, diced
- 2 cups wild Mushrooms slices
- 4 tablespoons grated parmesan cheese
- 1 tablespoon butter
- ½ teaspoon thyme
- ¼ teaspoon oregano
- 1 teaspoon minced garlic

How to make it:

1. Heat the oil in the instant pot.
2. Add the onions and cook for 3 minutes.
3. Add garlic and cook for 30 more seconds.
4. Stir in the mushroom slices and cook for 3-5 minutes.
5. Add the remaining ingredients, except the cheese.
6. Give the mixture a stir so you can combine everything well.
7. Close the lid and cook for five minutes on HIGH.
8. Do a quick pressure release.
9. Serve topped with the parmesan cheese.
10. Enjoy!

Tasty Cauliflower Riz:

Serves: 8
Total Time: 12 minutes
Macros per serving:
Calories: 161
Protein: 3.1 grams
Fat: 16.1 grams
Carbohydrates: 4.1 grams

What you'll need:

- 2 medium heads of cauliflower, cut into chunks
- 4 tablespoons olive oil
- ½ teaspoon salt
- 1 teaspoon dried parsley
- ½ teaspoon cumin
- ½ teaspoon turmeric
- ½ teaspoon paprika
- Fresh cilantro

How to make it:

1. Pour a cup of water into the insert of the moment pot.
2. Place the steamer trivet inside.
3. Arrange the cauliflower chunks over the trivet.
4. Secure the lid and select the "MANUAL" function with high pressure for 2 minutes.
5. After the beep, do a quick release and remove the lid.
6. Remove the chunks and empty the instant pot.
7. Add the oil and cooked cauliflower into the cooker. Press the "sauté" function key.
8. Use a potato masher to the cauliflower well.
9. Stir all told the remaining ingredients and "sauté" for five minutes.
10. Serve with cilantro on top.

Collard Greens with Balsamic Vinegar:

Serves: 4
Total Time: 30 minutes
Macros per serving:
Calories: 122
Protein: 4 grams
Fat: 7 grams
Carbohydrates: 12 grams

What you'll need:

- ½ teaspoon of salt
- 1 tablespoon of balsamic vinegar
- 3 cloves of garlic, minced
- 5 drops liquid stevia
- 1 small onion, thinly sliced
- 2 tablespoons of tomatoes, diced or 2 tablespoons of tomatoes puree
- 2 tablespoons of olive oil
- ½ cup of chicken broth
- 1 bunch of fresh collard greens, washed and soaked, chopped into small pieces

How to make it:

1. On the instant pot, select sauté. Add the olive oil, garlic, onion, chicken broth, vinegar, and tomato. Stir thoroughly.
2. On a separate bowl, place the chopped greens and mix it with some salt. Add stevia. Then add it into the pot, making sure all the greens are coated well sure all greens are coated well with the oil mixture.
3. Cook on manual for 20 minutes. Once done, do a quick pressure release.

Nicely Flavored Swiss Chard:

Serves: 6
Total Time: 13 minutes
Macros per serving:
Calories: 50
Protein: 0.9 grams
Fat: 4.8 grams
Carbohydrates: 0.31 grams

What you'll need:

- 2 ribs remove and chopped into bite-sized pieces large heads Swiss chard
- 2 tablespoons extra virgin olive oil
- ¼ teaspoon ground cumin
- 1/8 teaspoon crushed red pepper flakes
- 1/8 teaspoon cayenne pepper
- 1/3 cup water

How to make it:

1. In the pot of instant pot, add all ingredients and stir to combine.
2. Secure the lid and place the pressure valve to "seal" position.
3. Select "MANUAL" and cook beneath "High Pressure" for regarding three minutes.
4. Select the "CANCEL" and punctiliously do a natural unleash.
5. Remove the lid and serve.

A Different Ratatouille:

Serves: 4
Total Time: 20 minutes
Macros per serving:
Calories: 180
Protein: 2.5 grams
Fat: 10 grams
Carbohydrates: 6.5 grams

What you'll need:

- 1 ½ large zucchini
- 1 ½ large eggplant
- 3 large tomatoes, sliced
- 1 teaspoon minced garlic
- 1 tablespoon olive oil
- Salt and pepper, to taste
- 1 ½ cups water

How to make it:

1. Pour the water in your instant pot and lower the trivet.
2. Grease a round baking dish with cooking spray.
3. Arrange a layer of zucchini slices to cover the bottom of the dish. Then top with a layer of eggplant slices, and finally a layer of diced tomatoes. Repeat until you have no more ingredients left.
4. Drizzle the veggies with olive oil
5. Sprinkle with the garlic, and some salt and pepper.
6. Place the dish in the IP and close the lid.
7. Cook on HIGH for 10 minutes.
8. Serve and enjoy!

Wine-glazed Mushrooms:

Serves: 6
Total Time: 11 minutes
Macros per serving:
Calories: 91
Protein: 5 grams
Fat: 6.4 grams
Carbohydrates: 4.1 grams

What you'll need:

- 2 tablespoons olive oil
- 6 garlic cloves, minced
- 2 lbs. fresh mushrooms, sliced
- 1/3 cup balsamic vinegar
- 1/3 cup white wine
- Salt to taste
- Black pepper to taste

How to make it:

1. Add the oil and garlic to the instant pot and select the "sauté" function to cook for 1 minute.
2. Now add all the remaining ingredients to the cooker.
3. Switch the cooker to the "MANUAL" function with high pressure and 5 minutes cooking time.
4. After it is done, do a quick release then remove the lid.
5. Sprinkle some salt and black pepper if desired then serve.

Spaghetti Squash with Sage Garlic Sauce:

Serves: 4
Total Time: 25 minutes
Macros per serving:
Calories: 87
Protein: 2 grams
Fat: 7 grams
Carbohydrates: 11 grams

What you'll need:

- 1/8 teaspoon of nutmeg
- 1 teaspoon of salt
- 2 tablespoons of olive oil
- 4 cloves of garlic, sliced
- 1 small bunch fresh sage
- 1 cup of water
- 1 medium alimentary paste squash, cut in 0.5 and seeds removed

How to make it:

1. Add the water to the instant pot and place the squash at the bottom. Seal the lid and cook on manual for 3 to 4 minutes.
2. Meanwhile, in a separate pan, sauté the garlic and sage on olive oil. Pay attention to the pan to make sure the sage leaves are fried. They should be dark green and crispy.
3. Once the squash is done the cooking, do a quick pressure release. Pull the squash pressure release. Pull the squash fibers out of the shower and add them to the sauté pan.
4. After transfer, all the squash onto the pan, turn off heat and season with salt and nutmeg.
5. Stir well to incorporate ingredients and top with cheese before serving.

American Style Kale:

Serves: 4
Total Time: 17 minutes
Macros per serving:
Calories: 90
Protein: 3.6 grams
Fat: 12.7 grams
Carbohydrates: 3.17 grams

What you'll need:

- 1 tablespoon olive oil
- 3 slivered garlic cloves
- 1 pound trimmed and chopped fresh kale
- ½ cup water
- Salt and freshly ground black pepper, to taste
- 1 tablespoon fresh lemon juice

How to make it:

1. Place the oil within the instant pot and choose "sauté". Then add the garlic and cook for concerning one minute.
2. Add the kale and cook for concerning 1-2 minutes.
3. Select the "CANCEL" and stir in water, salt, and black pepper.
4. Secure the lid and place the pressure valve to "seal" position.
5. Select "MANUAL" and cook underneath "High Pressure" for concerning five minutes.
6. Select the "CANCEL" and thoroughly do a fast unleash.
7. Remove the lid and stir in lemon juice.
8. Serve hot.

Vegetarian Burger Patties:

Serves: 3
Total Time: 20 minutes
Macros per serving:
Calories: 148
Protein: 4 grams
Fat: 4 grams
Carbohydrates: 4.5 grams

What you'll need:

- 1 zucchini, chopped
- 1 cup cauliflower florets
- 1 cup broccoli florets
- ½ cup almond flour
- 1 egg
- ½ teaspoon minced garlic
- ½ onion, diced
- 1 teaspoon cumin
- ¼ teaspoon pepper
- ¼ teaspoon salt
- 1 tablespoon olive oil
- 1 ½ cups water

How to make it:

1. Place the veggies, egg, flour, and spices, in a food processor.
2. Process until ground.
3. Make 3 patties out of the mixture.
4. Heat the oil in your instant pot and cook the patties until golden on all side.
5. Transfer to a baking dish that has been previously greased.
6. Pour the water in your instant pot and lower the trivet.
7. Place the dish inside and close the lid.
8. Let cook for 5 minutes on HIGH.
9. Do a quick pressure release.
10. Serve and enjoy!

Asparagus Sticks:

Serves: 3
Total Time: 13 minutes
Macros per serving:
Calories: 164
Protein: 17.6 grams
Fat: 9.7 grams
Carbohydrates: 4.6 grams

What you'll need:

- 1 cup water
- 8 oz. thinly sliced prosciutto*
- 1 lb. thick asparagus sticks
- Salt to taste
- Pepper to taste

How to make it:

1. Warp each prosciutto slices over the asparagus sticks.
2. Pour a cup of water into the moment pot.
3. Arrange a steamer trivet inside.
4. Place the wrapped asparagus sticks over the trivet.
5. Secure the lid and select the "MANUAL" with high pressure for 3 minutes.
6. After the beep, do a natural release then remove the lid.
7. Transfer the steamed asparagus sticks to the platter
8. Sprinkle salt and pepper then serve.

Kale-Cabbage Broccoli Slaw:

Serves: 6
Total Time: 15 minutes
Macros per serving:
Calories: 97
Protein: 2 grams
Fat: 7 grams
Carbohydrates: 7 grams

What you'll need:

- ¼ cup of chopped kale
- ½ head of cabbage, thinly sliced
- 2 cups broccoli slaw
- 4 tablespoons of water
- 1 teaspoon of salt
- ¼ teaspoon of pepper

How to make it:

1. On the instant pot, pressure the sauté button. Add all the ingredients in.
2. Stir-fry 8-10 minutes or until cabbage softens to your liking.
3. Serve warm.

Super-Food Casserole:

Serves: 8
Cooking time: 35 minutes
Macros per serving:
Calories: 195
Protein: 11.4 grams
Fat: 14.3 grams
Carbohydrates: 0.81 grams

What you'll need:

- 6 orange eggs
- ½ cup heavy cream
- Salt and freshly ground black pepper, to taste
- 1 cup shredded cheddar cheese
- 2 ½ cups trimmed and chopped fresh kale
- 1 chopped small yellow onion
- 1 teaspoon herbs de Provence

How to make it:

1. In a large bowl, add eggs, heavy cream, salt, and black pepper and beat until well combined.
2. Add remaining ingredients and mix well.
3. Place the mixture into a baking dish evenly.
4. In the bottom of the instant pot, arrange a steamer trivet and pour 1 cup of water.
5. Place the dish on top of the trivet.
6. Secure the lid and place the pressure valve to "seal" position.
7. Select "MANUAL" and cook underneath "High Pressure" for regarding twenty minutes.
8. Select the "CANCEL" and punctiliously do a natural unharness.
9. Remove the lid and serve immediately.

Greek Keto Pasta:

Serves: 4
Total Time: 15 minutes
Macros per serving:
Calories: 230
Protein: 6.4 grams
Fat: 20 grams
Carbohydrates: 6.5 grams

What you'll need:

- 1 cup spinach
- ¼ cup parmesan cheese
- 10 kalamata olives
- 2 tablespoons butter
- ¼ cup crumbled feta cheese
- 2 tablespoons capers
- 2 large zucchini, spiralized
- 2 teaspoons minced garlic
- ¼ cup chopped sun-dried tomatoes
- 1 cup veggie broth

How to make it:

1. Melt the butter in your instant pot and cook the garlic for one minute.
2. Add noodles and spinach and cook for 1 minute.
3. Pour the broth over along with the remaining ingredients.
4. Close the lid and cook for three minutes on MANUAL.
5. Drain the pasta and serve.
6. Serve and enjoy!

Soups and Stews Recipes

Mom Approved Instant Pot Chicken Soup:

Serves: 6
Total Time: 45 minutes
Macros per serving:
Calories: 455
Protein: 29 grams
Fat: 32 grams
Carbohydrates: 11 grams

What you'll need:

- 2 tablespoons of butter (or avocado oil, if available)
- 6 chicken thighs
- 1 medium onion, diced
- 3 celery ribs, chopped
- 3 carrots, chopped
- 2 cloves of garlic, chopped
- 4 cups of chicken broth
- 2 cups filtered water
- 1 A teaspoon of parsley, diced
- 1 teaspoon of thyme, dried
- 2 teaspoons of kosher salt
- 1 teaspoon of pepper

How to make it:

1. Choose the sauté function on the instant pot. Add the butter. Place the chicken in batches on the pot. Cook each side for 2 minutes. Remove and set aside.
2. Put additional butter or oil, if necessary, to sauté the onion, celery, and carrots. Once the onion begins to soften, add garlic.
3. Turn off the instant pot. Place the chicken meat on top of the sautéed vegetables. Add the chicken broth, water, parsley, thyme, salt, and pepper. Cover with the lid and turn the pot's vent to Closed.
4. Choose the soup function on the instant pot. Allow 20-30 minutes to cook all the ingredients. Once done, release the pressure gently through the vent.
5. Remove the chicken, shred each thigh, and remove the bones. Place the shredded chicken back into the pot.

Staple Chicken Soup:

Serves: 8
Total Time: 45 minutes
Macros per serving:
Calories: 354
Protein: 47.6 grams
Fat: 11.9 grams
Carbohydrates: 1 gram

What you'll need:

- 2 ½ pounds grass-fed boneless, skinless chicken thighs
- 1 (10-ounce) can sugar-free diced tomatoes and green chills
- 1 (14 ½ -ounce) can sugar-free diced tomatoes
- 10 –ounce frozen mix veggie (yellow onion, celery, bell pepper)
- 8 cups homemade chicken broth
- 2 teaspoons chili powder
- Salt and freshly ground black pepper, to taste
- ½ cup chopped fresh cilantro

How to make it:

1. In the pot of instant pot, add all ingredients except cilantro and stir to combine.
2. Secure the lid and place the pressure valve to "seal" position.
3. Select the "soup" and simply use the default time of twenty-five minutes.
4. Select the "CANCEL" and punctiliously do a "Natural" unleash.
5. Remove the lid and with a slotted spoon, transfer the chicken thighs into a bowl.
6. With 2 forks, shred chicken thighs and then return to the pot.
7. Stir in cilantro and serve immediately.

Tomato and Basil Soup:

Serves: 4
Total Time: 30 minutes
Macros per serving:
Calories: 100
Protein: 2 grams
Fat: 4.5 grams
Carbohydrates: 9.2 grams

What you'll need:

- ½ onion, diced
- 28 ounces canned tomatoes
- 2 tablespoons tomato paste
- A handful of basil, chopped
- 1 tablespoon olive oil
- 3 cups veggie broth
- 1 teaspoon balsamic vinegar

How to make it:

1. Heat the oil in your IP on SAUTE.
2. Add onions and cook for 3 minutes.
3. Stir in the tomato paste and cook for one more minute.
4. Add tomatoes and broth.
5. Close the lid and choose SOUP mode.
6. Cook for 10 minutes.
7. Let the pressure release naturally.
8. Stir within the vinegar and 1/2 the basil.
9. Blend the soup with a hand blender.
10. Top with the remaining basil.
11. Serve and enjoy!

Delectable Chicken Soup:

Serves: 4
Total Time: 45 minutes
Macros per serving:
Calories: 805
Protein: 124.1 grams
Fat: 34 grams
Carbohydrates: 2.5 grams

What you'll need:

- 1 ½ pound grass-fed, boneless, skinless chicken thighs
- ½ (10-oz) can sugar-free diced tomatoes and green chilies
- ½ (14 ½ -oz.) can sugar-free diced tomatoes
- 5 oz. frozen mix veggies (yellow onion, celery. Bell pepper)
- 4 cups homemade chicken broth
- 1 teaspoon chili powder
- ½ teaspoon garlic powder
- Salt and freshly ground black pepper to taste

How to make it:

1. Put all the ingredients to the instant pot and secure the lid.
2. Select the "soup" function on your cooker and set the timer to 25 minutes.
3. After the beep, use 'natural release' to vent the steam, and then remove the lid.
4. Removed the chicken thighs and shred them using two forks.
5. Return the chicken to the pot and serve hot.

Creamy Cauliflower Soup:

Serves: 6
Total Time: 45 minutes
Macros per serving:
Calories: 325
Protein: 15 grams
Fat: 24 grams
Carbohydrates: 8.22 grams

What you'll need:

- 6 slices of bacon, chopped
- ¼ cup of onion, chopped
- 2 cloves of garlic, minced
- 1 stalk of celery, chopped
- Salt and pepper to taste
- 3 cups of chicken broth
- 1 head of cauliflower, cut into florets
- ¾ cup of sour cream
- 1 ½ cups cheddar cheese, shredded, divided
- 1 green onion

How to make it:

1. Choose the sauté function on the instant pot. Sauté the bacon until crisp. Stir frequently. Remove and put aside on a paper towel-lined plate. Leave the bacon fat in the pot.
2. Add the onion, garlic, and celery. Add salt and pepper for seasoning. Cook until the celery is softened. Turn off the sauté function on the pot.
3. Add the chicken broth and cauliflower. Lock the lid, seal the vent, select the manual function and set the pot's time for 5-10 minutes.
4. When the pot beeps, permit the pressure to unharness naturally for ten minutes. Open the vent and then remove the lid.
5. Add the sour cream and half of the shredded cheese. Stir thoroughly to blend well.
6. Pour the mixture into an immersion blender or food processor and blend until smooth.
7. Top with the remaining cheese, bacon, and green onion before serving. Serve hot.

Mexican Dinner Soup:

Serves: 8
Total Time: 30 minutes
Macros per serving:
Calories: 395
Protein: 40 grams
Fat: 20.5 grams
Carbohydrates: 1.6 grams

What you'll need:

- 2 pounds grass-fed boneless, skinless chicken breasts
- 1 (15-ounce) jar salsa
- 1 (4-ounce) can diced chilies
- 2 tablespoons ground cumin
- 1 tablespoon red chili powder
- 1 teaspoon garlic powder
- Salt and freshly ground black, to taste
- 5 cups homemade chicken broth
- 1 cup water
- 1 (8-ounce) block softened and chopped cream cheese

How to make it:

1. In the pot of instant pot, add all ingredients except cream cheese and stir to combine.
2. Secure the lid and place the pressure valve to "seal" position.
3. Select "MANUAL" and cook beneath "High Pressure" for regarding quarter-hour.
4. Select the "CANCEL" and thoroughly do a "Natural" unleash for regarding ten minutes and so do a "Quick" unleash.
5. Remove the lid and with a slotted spoon, transfer the chicken thighs into a bowl.
6. With 2 forks, shred chicken thighs and then return to the pot.
7. Now, select "sauté" and stir in cream cheese.
8. Cook for about 1-2 minutes, stirring continuously.
9. Select the "CANCEL" and serve hot.

Chicken and Spinach Soup:

Serves: 4
Total Time: 40 minutes
Macros per serving:
Calories: 180
Protein: 24 grams
Fat: 2.2 grams
Carbohydrates: 4 grams

What you'll need:

- 1 pound chicken, chopped
- 1 teaspoon garlic powder
- ½ onion, diced
- 1 cup spinach
- ½ fennel bulb, chopped
- 2 cups chicken broth
- 4 green onions, chopped
- Salt and pepper, to taste

How to make it:

1. Place everything in your instant pot.
2. Stir to combine the ingredients well.
3. Close the lid and choose the SOUP cooking mode.
4. Cook for 30 minutes.
5. Release the pressure naturally.
6. Serve and enjoy!

Full Meal Turkey Soup:

Serves: 3
Total Time: 45 minutes
Macros per serving:
Calories: 190
Protein: 19.5 grams
Fat: 9.7 grams
Carbohydrates: 6.2 grams

What you'll need:

- ½ tablespoon olive oil
- ½ lb. lean ground turkey
- ½ small yellow onion, chopped
- 1 cup carrots, peeled and shredded
- ¼ head cabbage, chopped
- 2 cups homemade chicken broth
- 2 teaspoons low-sodium soy sauce
- ½ teaspoon ground ginger
- Freshly ground black pepper to taste

How to make it:

1. Place the oil and turkey in the instant pot and select the "sauté" function to cook for 5 minutes.
2. Select "CANCEL" then add the remaining ingredients. Cover and lock the lid.
3. Set the cooker to "MANUAL" and select high pressure for 25 minutes.
4. After the completion beep, 'Quick Release' the steam and then remove the lid.
5. Serve hot.

Taste Of India Cream of Broccoli Soup:

Serves: 6
Total Time: 30 minutes
Macros per serving:
Calories: 125
Protein: 4 grams
Fat: 15 grams
Carbohydrates: 12 grams

What you'll need:

- 2 tablespoons of coconut oil(or olive oil)
- 2 medium shallots, chopped
- 3 medium leeks (white parts only), cleaned, trimmed, and chopped
- 1 tablespoon of Indian curry powder
- Kosher salt to taste a ¼ cup of apple, peeled and diced
- 1 ½ lb. of broccoli, chopped florets
- 4 cups of chicken stock
- Black pepper to taste, freshly ground
- 1 cup of full-fat coconut milk
- Optional: leftover pork meat, crisped
- Optional: chives for garnish

How to make it:

1. Select the sauté function on the instant pot. Add coconut oil once the pot is hot.
2. Sauté the shallots, leeks, curry powder, and salt. Cook for about 5 minutes. Stir often.
3. Add the apple and broccoli. Mix well.
4. Add the broth. Add water if desired but make sure you only fill 2/3 of the pot.
5. Press the cancel/to keep warm. Press High pressure and set the pot's timer for 5 minutes. Cover and allow cooking.
6. When done, turn off the pot and manually release the pressure.
7. Transfer the soup to a food processor. Blitz the soup until it becomes a smooth and aromatic puree.
8. Add coconut milk, salt, and pepper. Blend well. Garnish with pork and chives, if desired, before serving.

Flavor-Packed Soup:

Serves: 6
Total Time: 50 minutes
Macros per serving:
Calories: 513
Protein: 22.1 grams
Fat: 45.1 grams
Carbohydrates: 0.88 grams

What you'll need:

- 6 grass-fed cubed boneless, skinless chicken thighs
- 6-ounces sliced fresh mushrooms
- ½ cup chopped frozen onion
- ½ cup chopped frozen celery
- 4 minced garlic cloves
- 8-ounce softened cream cheese
- ¼ cup softened butter
- 1 teaspoon dried thyme
- Salt and freshly ground black pepper, to taste
- 3 cups homemade chicken broth
- 1 cup heavy cream
- 2 cups fresh spinach
- 1 cup chopped cooked bacon

How to make it:

1. In the pot of instant pot, add all ingredients except cream, spinach, and bacon and stir to combine.
2. Secure the lid and place the pressure valve to "seal" position.
3. Select the "soup" and simply use the default time of half-hour.
4. Select the "CANCEL" and thoroughly do a "Natural" unleash.
5. Remove the lid and stir in cream and spinach.
6. Immediately, secure the lid for about 10 minutes.
7. Top with bacon and serve.

No-Fuss Lamb Stew:

Serves: 5
Total Time: 50minutes
Macros per serving:
Calories: 274
Protein: 3 grams
Fat: 19 grams
Carbohydrates: 9 grams

What you'll need:

- 2 pounds of lamb stew meat, cubed
- 1 acorn squash, peeled, seeded, cubed
- 3 large yellow onion, sliced into half moons
- 1 large yellow onion, sliced into half moons
- 6 cloves of garlic, sliced
- 1 sprig of rosemary
- 1 bay leaf
- ½ teaspoon of salt
- 3 tablespoons of broth

How to make it:

1. Place all ingredients into the instant pot. Select the soup or stew function. Set the pot's timer for 35 minutes.
2. Once done, quick release the pressure. Unlock the lid after 5-10 minutes.

Lamb Stew:

Serves: 8
Total Time: 85-90 minutes
Macros per serving:
Calories: 462
Protein: 30 grams
Fat: 37 grams
Carbohydrates: 1.2 grams

What you'll need:

- ½ cup lamb tallow
- 3 cloves garlic crushed
- 1 large onion(diced)
- ¼ cup rosemary (chopped)
- 3 sticks celery (diced)
- 1 teaspoon salt
- 1 teaspoon ground black pepper
- ½ cup red wine vinegar
- 1 cup tomato puree
- 4 cups beef broth
- 4 lbs. lamb shoulder (cut into 1 ½ inch chunks)
- ½ lbs. mushrooms (cut into ½ inch sliced)
- 1 cup sour cream
- ½ cup parmesan cheese

How to make it:

1. Place the tallow, garlic, onions, rosemary in the instant pot. Set the instant pot to "sauté" and cook for 5 minutes stirring occasionally.
2. Add the salt, pepper, vinegar and tomato puree and cook for another 5 minutes stirring occasionally.
3. Add the beef broth, mix well and then add lamb chunks. If needed add water enough that lamb is just covered.
4. Place and lock the lid set the instant pot to "meat/stew" and cooking time to 60 minutes.
5. When done let to naturally release the pressure.
6. Set the instant pot to "sauté" and add to it sliced mushrooms, and cook for 15 minutes.
7. Serve hot, topped with 2 tablespoons of sour cream and one tablespoon of grated parmesan cheese.

Simple Beef Stew:

Serves: 4
Total Time: 40 minutes
Macros per serving:
Calories: 363
Protein: 30 grams
Fat: 32 grams
Carbohydrates: 6 grams

What you'll need:

- 1 pound beef, chopped into cubes
- 28 ounce diced canned tomatoes, undrained
- 3 cups beef broth
- 1 carrot, sliced
- ½ onion, diced
- 2 teaspoons minced garlic
- 1 red bell pepper, diced
- 1 bay leaf
- 1 teaspoon thyme
- 1 tablespoon olive oil
- 2 tablespoons chopped parsley

How to make it:

1. Heat the oil in your instant pot on SAUTE.
2. Sauté the onions and peppers for 3 minutes.
3. Add garlic and thyme and cook for another.
4. Add the beef and cook until browned.
5. Stir in the remaining ingredients.
6. Close the lid and choose the MANUAL cooking mode.
7. Cook on HIGH for 20 minutes.
8. Wait five minutes before doing a fast pressure unleash.
9. Serve and enjoy!

Lamb pepper Stew:

Serves: 3
Total Time: 45 minutes
Macros per serving:
Calories: 252
Protein: 33.1 grams
Fat: 10.4 grams
Carbohydrates: 5.3 grams

What you'll need:

- ½ tablespoon olive oil
- ½ small yellow onion, chopped
- ½ celery stalk, chopped
- ½ tablespoon garlic, minced
- 1 lb. grass-fed lamb shoulder, trimmed and cubed into 2-inch size
- 1 cup fresh tomatoes, chopped finely
- 1 tablespoon sugar-free tomato paste
- 1 ½ tablespoon fresh lemon juice
- ½ teaspoon dried oregano, crushed
- ½ teaspoon dried basil, crushed
- Salt and freshly ground black pepper to taste
- ¼ cup homemade chicken broth
- ½ large green bell pepper, seeded and cut into 8 slices
- ½ large red bell pepper, seeded and cut into 8 slices
- ¼ cup fresh parsley, minced

How to make it:

1. Add the oil, onion, and garlic to the instant pot and select "sauté". Cook for 2 minutes.
2. Now add all the remaining ingredients and secure the lid.
3. Select the 'MANUAL' function and cook for 15 minutes on high pressure.
4. After the beep, use 'natural release' for 10 minutes, then vent any remaining steam by using 'quick release'
5. Remove the lid and switch the cooker back to the 'sauté' mode.
6. Add the bell peppers and cook for 8 minutes stirring constantly.
7. Garnish with minced parsley and serve.

Chicken, Tomato, And Kale Stew:

Serves: 4
Total Time: 55 minutes
Macros per serving:
Calories: 132
Protein: 13 grams
Fat: 10 grams
Carbohydrates: 7 grams

What you'll need:

- 1 tablespoon of butter
- ½ onion, chopped
- 2 boneless chicken breasts, diced
- 3 cups of kale, chopped
- 15 ounces. Of diced tomatoes
- 1 cup of chicken broth
- ½ teaspoon of garlic powder
- ½ teaspoon of oregano
- ½ teaspoon of salt
- ¼ teaspoon of black pepper, ground

How to make it:

1. Choose the sauté function on the instant pot. Melt the butter and sauté the onion for concerning three minutes.
2. Add the chicken. Cook for 5 minutes, stirring a few times until the chicken is golden brown.
3. Add the kale, tomatoes, chicken broth, garlic powder, oregano, salt, and black pepper. Close the lid.
4. Select high pressure on the pot. Set the pot's timer for 10 minutes. It will take 10-15 minutes for the pressure to build.
5. Once done, naturally release the pressure for 10 minutes. Afterward, quick-release any remaining pressure.
6. After 5 minutes, unlock, remove the lid, and serve.

CONCLUSION:

Thank you for reading this book and having the patience to try the recipes.

I do hope that you gain as much enjoyment reading and experimenting with the meals as I have had writing these books.
If you would like to leave a comment, you can do it at the Order section->Digital order send and also buy paperback, in your Amazon account.

Stay safe and healthy!

Made in the USA
Middletown, DE
13 February 2020